W9-CFI-167

TIME
ANNUAL
2006

TIME ANNUAL 2006

EDITOR	Kelly Knauer
DESIGNER	Ellen Fanning
PICTURE EDITOR	Patricia Cadley
WRITER/RESEARCH DIRECTOR	Matthew McCann Fenton
COPY EDITOR	Bruce Christopher Carr

TIME INC. HOME ENTERTAINMENT

PUBLISHER	Richard Fraiman
EXECUTIVE DIRECTOR, MARKETING SERVICES	Carol Pittard
DIRECTOR, RETAIL & SPECIAL SALES	Tom Mifsud
MARKETING DIRECTOR, BRANDED BUSINESSES	Swati Rao
DIRECTOR, NEW PRODUCT DEVELOPMENT	Peter Harper
FINANCIAL DIRECTOR	Steven Sandonato
PREPRESS MANAGER	Emily Rabin
BOOK PRODUCTION MANAGER	Jonathan Polsky
MARKETING MANAGER	Kristin Treadway
ASSOCIATE PREPRESS MANAGER	Anne-Michelle Gallero

SPECIAL THANKS TO

Bozena Bannett, Alexandra Bliss, Glenn Buonocore, Barbara Dudley Davis, Brian Fellows, Suzanne Janso, Robert Marasco, Brooke McGuire, Chavaughn Raines, Ilene Schreider, Adriana Tierno, Brooke Twyford, Britney Williams

Copyright 2005 Time Inc. Home Entertainment
Published by TIME Books
Time Inc. • 1271 Avenue of the Americas • New York, NY 10020

All rights reserved. No part of this book may be reproduced in any form or by any electronic or mechanical means, including information storage and retrieval systems, without permission in writing from the publisher, except by a reviewer, who may quote brief passages in a review. TIME and the Red Border Design are protected through trademark registration in the United States and in the foreign countries where TIME magazine circulates.

First Edition • ISBN: 1-932994-69-6 ISSN: 1097-5721
TIME Books is a trademark of Time Inc.

We welcome your comments and suggestions about TIME Books. Please write to us at
TIME Books • Attention: Book Editors • PO Box 11016 • Des Moines, IA 50336-1016

If you would like to order any of our hardcover Collector's Edition books, please call us at 1-800-327-6388
(Monday through Friday, 7 a.m.–8 p.m., or Saturday, 7 a.m.–6 p.m., Central time).

PRINTED IN THE UNITED STATES OF AMERICA

TIME
ANNUAL

THESE HONORED DEAD: Robby Herbolt and fellow Boy Scouts in Union Township, Ohio, established a memorial field to recognize the U.S. troops who have died since 2001 in Iraq and Afghanistan. On Jan. 25, 2005, when this picture was taken, the toll of U.S. dead in Iraq was 1,368. In late October the death count reached a milestone when it passed 2,000

2006

CONTENTS

OUT ON A LIMB: Hurled by Hurricane Katrina's winds, a seafood-delivery truck gets arboreal in Empire, La., near the mouth of the Mississippi River

TIME ANNUAL 2006

KADIR VAN LOHUIZEN—AGENCE VU

Semper Fi

In the predawn hours of Jan. 26, 2005, a U.S. Super Stallion transport helicopter crashed in a fierce sandstorm in western Iraq, killing 30 Marines and a Navy sailor. It was the U.S. military's largest loss of life in a single incident since American troops moved into Iraq in March 2003. In a memorial service attended by 500 Marines on Feb. 2, the men's boots, helmets and rifles recalled their service; a Marine who played a guitar before the formal service began left it on display. The young soldiers who died had taken part in the bitter fighting for insurgent-held Fallujah in November 2004; they were moving to Camp Korean Village, near the town of Rutbah, to help ensure security for the Jan. 30 Iraqi national elections. "These were brave men who had served their country with honor," said commanding officer Colonel W. Lee Miller. "We will hold the memories of these fallen warriors close to our hearts forever."

**ANJA NIEDRINGHAUS—
AP/WIDE WORLD**

Camp Korean Village, Anbar Province, Iraq, February 2

Life in the Balance

Hurricane Katrina wreaked its worst damage along the Gulf Coast towns of Mississippi. Residents who had weathered previous storms said that Katrina's ferocious winds were much more intense than they had seen before. The hurricane's massive storm surge was equally unprecedented in size; it produced flash floods that swamped streets and houses, driving homeowners to their attics and roofs. At right, members of the Taylor family tried to evacuate the Bay St. Louis area but were caught up in the floods and retreated to the roof of their SUV, which provided only a temporary sanctuary. Members of the town's Emergency Management Agency successfully fought the waves and rescued the Taylors. Local first responders like these did an admirable job in the first hours after the storm struck, but federal agencies, which are supposed to provide ongoing support after the first 72 hours of a natural disaster, notoriously fumbled their response to Katrina.

BEN SKLAR—AP/WIDE WORLD

Bay St. Louis, Mississippi, August 29

The Wasteland

Freelance photographer Chris Usher, on assignment for TIME, drove to the Gulf Coast on Aug. 28, the day before Katrina made landfall; his was one of the few vehicles traveling south on that dismal day. Usher remained in the area for weeks, photographing scenes like this one that reveal the enormous devastation Katrina wrought along the Mississippi coast. Usher said, "I'm from the Midwest, and I've seen the damage tornadoes can do, carving out a narrow trail of destruction. But Katrina was like a 250-mile-wide tornado that turned the entire Mississippi coast into a wasteland." Here, Lauren Naulett and Kacey Moore search through the debris of their adoptive grandparents' home for any personal effects that might have survived the storm, 12 days after it reduced the house to rubble. They told Usher that because their grandfather Ben Wilkes was suffering from terminal cancer and could not visit the site, he had asked them to make this bitter pilgrimage.

CHRIS USHER FOR TIME

Gulfport, Mississippi, September 10

Pakistan's Pain

On Oct. 8, an earthquake of 7.6 magnitude struck Kashmir, the mountainous region between India and Pakistan that has long been the focus of a dispute between the two nations. The quake leveled entire villages, burying thousands of people, many of whose bodies may never be recovered. In Pakistan, more than 2 million people were left homeless and some 79,000 people were believed to have died, according to estimates in late October; the number was expected to grow. In the Indian section of Kashmir, the quake killed more than 1,300 and left more than 100,000 people without shelter. Although many nations dispatched aid to the region, rainstorms delayed rescuers, as did the sheer remoteness of many of the stricken towns. It took troops from Pakistan's army three days to arrive in Balakot, a town of 20,000 people that was reduced to a muddy smear by the quake, even though their base was only 20 miles away. When the soldiers finally arrived at a collapsed school building to help dig out some 200 students trapped inside, enraged parents hurled stones at the troops.

KATE BROOKS—POLARIS

Balakot, Kashmir, October 10

Murder Most Foul

In his two terms as Lebanon's Prime Minister, ending in October 2004, Rafiq Hariri helped his nation rebuild from the chaos and blight of a bloody civil war that lasted from 1975 to 1990. But the price of revival was steep: Hariri allowed neighboring Syria to station troops within Lebanon and boss its politics. During the tenure of the self-made billionaire—who built his fortune on construction, oil, real estate and banking— gleaming hotels and office towers sprang up along Beirut's Mediterranean shore. But it was there that a huge explosion blew apart Hariri's armor-plated convoy of cars on Feb. 14, killing Hariri and 14 others. At right, a bystander calls for help. Hariri's death galvanized Lebanon's anti-Syria opposition. After major street protests, President Bashar Assad withdrew Syria's 14,000 troops from Lebanon in April. In October a United Nations report implicated Assad's regime in the murder, specifically fingering the President's brother, Maher Assad, head of the Presidential Guard, and brother-in-law Assef Shawkat, chief of military intelligence. The U.S. hoped the report would help step up international pressure on Assad's regime, which it has long accused of destabilizing the region.

MOHAMED AZAKIR—REUTERS

Beirut, February 14

New York City, February 21

Orange Crush

For 16 days in February, New York City's Central Park was cinched with a saffron sash, thanks to veteran installation artists Christo and Jeanne-Claude, whose ambitious projects—such as the wrapping in fabric of Berlin's Reichstag, Paris' Pont Neuf and several islands in Miami's Biscayne Bay—have made them art-world superstars. Finally realizing a decades-old vision, the Bulgarian-born artist and his French-born wife decked the malls of the park with 7,503 orange "gates," with each unit standing 16 ft. high. If nothing else, the supersized serving of saffron proved that art resides in the eye of the beholder: many viewers thrilled to the ever shifting display, which conferred visibility on each gust of wind as it rippled across the gates, but other onlookers shared the view of radio pundit Rush Limbaugh, who dissed the project's components as "orange shower curtains." Not in doubt was the work's massive drawing power: some 4,000,000 people are estimated to have experienced the installation.

BETH A. KEISER—CORBIS

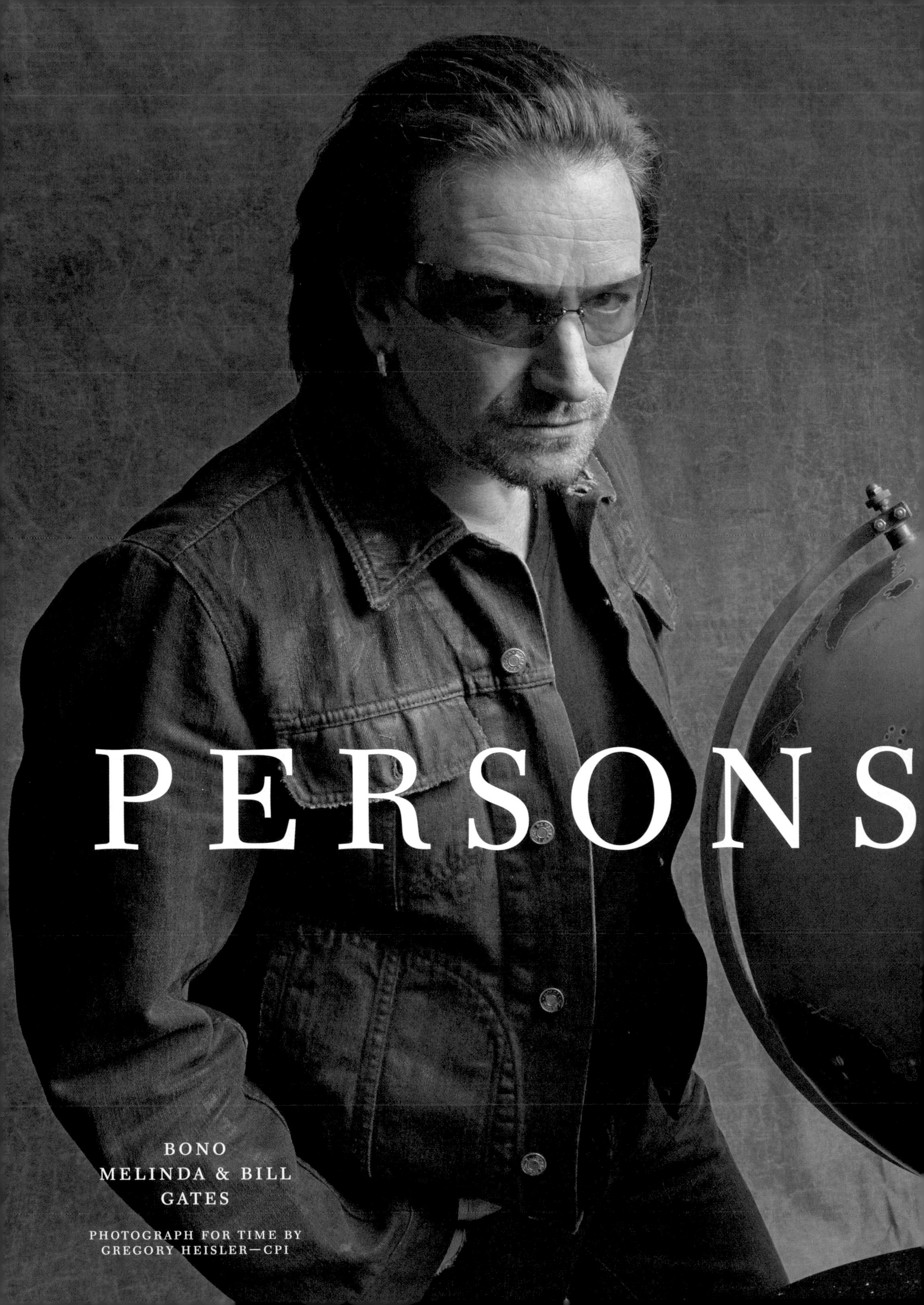

PERSONS

BONO
MELINDA & BILL
GATES

PHOTOGRAPH FOR TIME BY
GREGORY HEISLER—CPI

of the YEAR

By Nancy Gibbs

THESE ARE NOT THE PEOPLE YOU EXPECT TO COME TO THE RESCUE. ROCK STARS are designed to be shiny, shallow creatures, furloughed from reality for all time. Billionaires are even more removed, nestled atop fantastic wealth where they never again have to place their own calls or defrost dinner or fly commercial. So Bono spends several thousand dollars at a restaurant for a nice Pinot Noir, and Bill Gates, the great predator of the Internet age, has a trampoline room in his $100 million house. It makes you think that if these guys can decide to

TIME

make it their mission to save the world, partner with people they would never otherwise meet, care about causes that are not sexy or dignified in the ways that celebrities normally require, then no one really has a good excuse anymore for just staying on the sidelines and watching.

Such is the nature of Bono's fame that just about everyone in the world wants to meet him—except for the richest man in the world, who thought it would be a waste of time. "World health is immensely complicated," says Gates, recalling that first encounter in 2002. "It doesn't really boil down to a 'Let's be nice' analysis. So I thought a meeting wouldn't be all that valuable."

It took about three minutes with Bono for Gates to change his mind. Bill and his wife Melinda, another computer nerd turned poverty warrior, love facts and data with a tenderness most people reserve for their children, and Bono was hurling metrics across the table as fast as they could keep up. "He was every bit the geek that we are," says Gates Foundation chief Patty Stonesifer, who helped broker that first summit. "He just happens to be a geek who is a fantastic musician."

And so another alliance was born: unlikely, unsentimental, hard nosed, clear eyed and dead set on driving poverty into history. The rocker's job is to be raucous, grab our attention and bring us to our feet. The engineers' job is to make things work. 2005 is the year they turned the corner, when Bono charmed and bullied and morally blackmailed the leaders of the world's richest countries into forgiving $40 billion in debt owed by the poorest; now those countries can spend the money on health and schools rather than interest payments—and have no more excuses for not doing so.

The Gateses, having created the world's biggest charity, with a $29 billion endowment, spent the year giving more money away faster than anyone ever has, including nearly half a billion dollars for the Grand Challenges, in which they asked the very best brains in the world how they would solve a huge problem, like inventing a vaccine that needs no needles and no refrigeration, if they had the money to do it.

It would be easy to watch the alliance in action and imagine the division of labor: head and heart, business and culture; one side brings the money, the other side the buzz. But like many great teams, this one is more than the sum of its symbols. Apart from his music stardom, Bono is a busy capitalist (he's a named partner in a $2 billion private equity firm), moves in political circles like a very charming shark, aptly named his organization DATA (debt, AIDS, trade, Africa) to capture both the breadth of his ambitions and the depth of his research. Meanwhile, you could watch Bill and Melinda coolly calculate how many lives will be saved by each billion they spend and miss how impassioned they are about the suffering they have seen. "He's changing the world twice," says Bono of Bill. "And the second act for Bill Gates may be the one that history regards more."

For being shrewd about doing good, for rewiring politics and re-engineering justice, for making mercy smarter and hope strategic and then daring the rest of us to follow, Bill and Melinda Gates and Bono are TIME's Persons of the Year for 2005.

Through Different Windows

On a recent "learning tour" of India, Melinda and Bill Gates meet the Naik family in a slum outside Delhi. Melinda is holding Liza, who was born in this home a month earlier. "Lives were being treated as if they weren't valuable," the Microsoft co-founder once said. Gates knows value: for years he has been the wealthiest individual in the world

PHOTOGRAPH FOR TIME BY JAMES NACHTWEY—VII

AS IT HAPPENS, THEY HAVE ARRIVED AT THE RIGHT time, as America stirs itself awake from the dreamy indifference with which the world's poor have forever been treated. In ordinary times, we give when it's easy: a gesture, a reflex, a salve to conscience. The entreaties come on late-night TV from well-meaning but long-discarded celebrities who cuddle with big-eyed children and appeal to pity and guilt. Maybe we send off a check, hope it will help someone somewhere stay alive for another day. That is not the model for the current crusaders or the message for these extraordinary times.

This was already a year that redefined generosity. Americans gave more money to tsunami relief, more than $1.6 billion, than to any overseas mission ever before. The Hurricane Season from Hell along the Gulf Coast brought another outpouring of money and time and water bottles and offers of refuge, some $2.7 billion so far. The public failure of government to manage disaster became the political story of the year. But the private response of individuals, from lemonade stands to mitten drives, is the human story of 2005.

"Katrina created one tragedy and revealed another," Melinda Gates said in a speech after the hurricane. "We have to address the inequities that were not created by the hurricanes but exposed by them. We have to ensure that people have the opportunity to make the most of their lives." That just about captures the larger mission she and her husband have embraced. In the poorest countries, every day is as deadly as a hurricane. Malaria kills two African children a minute, round the clock. In that minute

In the Name of Love

Bono makes a new friend at a children's hospital in Cape Town, South Africa. The frontman for U2 is well aware that do-gooding celebrities are ripe for ridicule: "When an Irish rock star starts talking about [poverty], people go, yeah, you're paid to be indulged and have these ideas." But his charisma is coupled with a strong command of detail

RICHARD YOUNG—REX USA

a woman dies from complications during pregnancy, nine people get infected with HIV, three people die of TB. A vast host of aid workers and agencies and national governments and international organizations have struggled for years to get ahead of the problem but often fell behind. The task was too big, too complicated. There was no one in charge, no consensus about what to do first and never enough money to do it. How you cut an umbilical cord can determine whether a baby risks a fatal infection, but every culture has its own traditions. They cut with a coin for luck in Nepal and a stone in Bolivia, where they think if you use a razor blade the child will grow up to be a thief. There is no one solution to fit all countries, and so the model the Gates Foundation and Bono have embraced pulls in everyone, at every level. Think globally. Act carefully. Prove what works. Then use whatever levers you have to get it done.

The challenge of "stupid poverty"—the people who die for want of a $2 pill because they live on $1 a day—was enough to draw Gates away from Microsoft years before he intended to shift his focus from making money to giving it away. He and Melinda looked around and recognized a systems failure. "Those lives were being treated as if they weren't valuable," Gates told FORTUNE in 2002. "Well, when you have the resources that could make a very big impact, you can't just say to yourself, 'O.K., when I'm 60, I'll get around to that. Stand by.'"

There have always been rich and famous people who feel the call to "give back," which is where big marble buildings and opera houses come from. But Bill and Melinda didn't set out to win any prizes—or friends. "They've gone into international health," says Paul Farmer, a public-health pi-

oneer, "and said, 'What, are you guys kidding? Is this the best you can do?'" Gates' standards are shaping the charitable marketplace as he has the software universe. "He wants to know where every penny goes," says Bono, whose DATA got off the ground with a Gates Foundation grant. "Not because those pennies mean so much to him, but because he's demanding efficiency." His rigor has been a blessing to everyone—not least of all Bono, who was at particular risk of not being taken seriously, just another guilty white guy pestering people for more money without focusing on where it goes. "When an Irish rock star starts talking about it, people go, yeah, you're paid to be indulged and have these ideas," Bono says. "But when Bill Gates says you can fix malaria in 10 years, they know he's done a few spreadsheets."

The Gateses' commitment acts as a catalyst. They needed the drug companies to come on board, and the major health agencies, the churches, the universities and politicians who were raised to believe that foreign aid was about as politically sexy as postal reform. And that is where Bono comes in. He goes to churches and talks of Christ and the lepers, citing how many passages of Scripture ("2,103") deal with taking care of the poor; he sits in a corporate boardroom and talks about the role of aid in reviving the U.S. brand. He gets Pat Robertson and Susan Sarandon to do a commercial together for his ONE campaign to "Make Poverty History." Then he heads to Washington, where he stops by a meeting of House Democrats to nuzzle them about debt relief before a private lunch with President George W. Bush, whom he praises for tripling aid to Africa since 2001. Everyone from Republican Senator Rick Santorum to Hillary Clinton used a fall U2 concert in the capital as a fund raiser. "He knows how to get people to follow him," Stonesifer says. "We are probably a good complement. We're more likely to give you four facts about the disease than four ways that you can go do something about it."

Bono grasps that politicians don't much like being yelled at by activists who tell them no matter what they do, it's not enough. Bono knows it's never enough, but he also knows how to say so in a way that doesn't leave his audience feeling helpless. He invites everyone into the game, convincing them they are missing something if they hold back. "After so many years in Washington," says retired Senator Jesse Helms of North Carolina, whom Bono recruited to his cause, "I had met enough well-known people to quickly figure out who was genuine and who was there for show. I knew as soon as I met Bono that he was genuine. He has absolutely nothing to gain personally as a result of his work. In fact, he has opened himself to criticism because he has been willing to work with anyone to find help for these children who have taken his heart."

This is not about pity. It's more about passion. Pity sees suffering and wants to ease the pain; passion sees injustice and wants to settle the score. Pity implores the powerful to pay attention; passion warns them about what will happen if they don't. The risk of pity is that it kills with kindness; the promise of passion is that it builds on the hope that the poor are fully capable of helping themselves if given the chance. In 2005 the world's poor needed no more condolences; they needed people to get interested, get mad and then get to work. ∎

THE CONSTANT CHARMER

How the world's biggest rock star mastered the art of politics to fight global poverty

By Josh Tyrangiel

THE G-8 SUMMIT IS AN ANNUAL GATHERING of the world's most powerful individuals at which two things are always accomplished: an awkward group photo is taken and no one has any fun. On the July night that this year's summit began in Gleneagles, Scotland, Bono thought it might be nice to change things up a bit. U2 had scheduled a concert at a stadium in nearby Edinburgh, and Bono, as is his custom, invited pretty much everyone he thought would be interesting to drop by, which explains how George Clooney, Hollywood's leading lefty, and Paul Wolfowitz, president of the World Bank and an architect of the Iraq war, ended up in the same room backstage. "It could have been a little uncomfortable," says Clooney. "In fact, I was kind of expecting it to be."

A few minutes before U2 was due to perform, Bono strolled in and plopped himself down—not on the couch or near it but on top of it, like a household pet. Then he began talking about the one interest that Clooney, Wolfowitz and almost everyone else who had come to Scotland that day had in common: persuading developed nations to help lift 1 billion people out of extreme poverty. Bono's precise words on the subject are lost to history. "I couldn't stop looking at him," says Clooney. "He's so affectless. You felt like you're in the living room with your buddy who just happens to be a global rock star and has the world's best interests at heart." Says Wolfowitz: "Pomposity and arrogance are the enemies of getting things done. And Bono knows how to get things done."

Pleasant collisions happen a lot when Bono is around.

Ashley Judd mixes in the greenroom at a U2 show with Dean Kamen, inventor of the Segway scooter and an aborning machine that makes even the filthiest water drinkable. Bill Gates goes to a nightclub, gets called a "bad motherf_____" by Diddy and understands that it is intended as a compliment. Of course, if Bono were to rely solely on his ability to get powerful people in a room with famous people and then hit them with a speech about moral obligations, he would be little more than the lead singer in the war on global poverty—a nice title but limited in its power. "If you really want to be effective, you have to bring something to the table beyond just charisma," says Rick Santorum, conservative Republican Senator from Pennsylvania. "The important thing is, Bono understands his issues better than 99% of members of Congress."

Knowing the facts is crucial—"Everybody hates a dilettante," says Bono—but so is knowing your audience.

ON THE MOVE: Outside his Manhattan home, Bono prepares to head to another concert. He is never idle. "I'm like a camel," he says. "I store up sleep in my hump."
Photograph for TIME by Antonin Kratochvil—VII

When he lunches with President Bush, as he did most recently in October, Bono quotes Scripture and talks about small projects in Africa that have specific metrics for success. Then he asks for more money to fund them. In the office of Senator Dick Durbin, Democrat from Illinois, he speaks of multilateralism and how development aid reminds the rest of the world of America's greatness. Then he asks for more money. In stadiums, he tells people that if they join together, they have a chance to "make poverty history." Then U2 plays *One*.

Bono's great gift is to take what has made him famous—charm, clarity of voice, an ability to touch people in their secret heart—combine those traits with a keen grasp of the political game and obsessive attention to detail, and channel it all toward getting everyone, from world leaders to music lovers, to engage with something overwhelming in its complexity. Although it's tempting for some to cast his global road show as the vanity project of a pampered celebrity, the fact is that Bono gets results. At Gleneagles—where Bono and his policy-and-advocacy body, DATA, met with five of the eight heads of state at the summit—the G-8 approved an unprecedented $50 billion aid package—including $25 billion for Africa—and pledged near universal access to antiretroviral drugs for almost 10 million needy people who are HIV-positive.

Bono technically didn't achieve any of those things on his own, "but it's hard to imagine much of it would have been done without him," says Canadian Prime Minister Paul Martin. Although politicians, academics and activists continue to differ over the best way to tackle poverty and disease in the developing world, Bono's contribution has been to forge, over the past decade, a surprisingly durable consensus on the need to do *something*. "The only thing that balances how preposterous it is to have to listen to an Irish rock star talk about these subjects," says Bono, "is the weight of the subjects themselves."

Ballast is not an appurtenance commonly attributed to pop stars. Bono, 45, spends his evenings lifting people to their feet, but offstage, he can be almost aggressively grounded. A significant part of his charisma stems from the fact that he isn't intimidating. There are rock stars who enter a room with the kind of sex display the Discovery Channel saves for sweeps weeks, but Bono is not one of them. He's handsome but short—5 ft. 7 in. in thick-soled shoes—and swings his arms wide when he walks, so he looks open and soft, like a pillow in a cowboy hat. It's not at all what people expect, and it sets them at ease.

More than two decades since Bono came into view as U2's mullet-haired front man, he commands attention like no other cultural figure alive. When he visits Capitol Hill, his movement through the halls is split-timed. His lobbyists feed him tips so he knows, for instance, that Senator Mitch McConnell admires Burmese dissident Aung San

Then in 1997 he learned that although Live Aid raised $200 million, Ethiopia alone paid $500 million in annual debt service to the world's lending institutions. Bono soon signed on as a spokesman for Jubilee 2000, a church-based campaign born in Britain that asked governments to use the millennium as an occasion to cancel Third World debt. Bono, who spends most of his non-touring time in his hometown, Dublin, with Ali and their four children, started flying to Washington for weekends at the World Bank with his friend Bobby Shriver, a son of Eunice and Sargent Shriver. As he began to grapple with the levers of power, he learned from economist Jeffrey Sachs, even as he lobbied the Clinton White House and wooed both liberals like Nancy Pelosi and conservatives like John Kasich in the House.

When Bono decided he needed to get organized, Geldof, one of Bono's closest friends, came up with the name DATA, a double acronym meant to anchor the group as a nexus between the nonprofit development world

FRIENDS IN HIGH PLACES: BONO AND ... Bill Clinton, Bill Gates, Kofi Annan, Tony Blair, Nigeria's Olusegun Obasanjo ... Condoleezza Rice

Suu Kyi, a Nobel Peace Prize winner who inspired U2's song *Walk On*. Arriving with no security, Bono bears gifts: a leather-bound volume of Seamus Heaney for Senator Patrick Leahy, a framed copy of the Marshall Plan speech for Colin Powell. He poses for every staff picture; his thank-you notes are handwritten and prompt. He wears whatever. "I literally get into the clothes at the end of the bed," he says. "If somebody doesn't take them off and wash them, things would probably get a bit high."

TWENTY YEARS AGO, THE NOTION OF BONO AS A POLITICAL player was almost unimaginable. In 1985, U2 played Live Aid, the Bob Geldof–organized concert for African famine relief, deemed a success at the time. After the concert, Bono, born Paul Hewson, and his wife Ali Hewson spent six weeks working at an orphanage in Wello, Ethiopia. The weight of famine, war and corruption, as well as the resentment many Africans feel toward uninformed foreigners bearing messiah complexes, overwhelmed him. As did the foolishness of thinking a day of singing was enough. But U2 was on its way to becoming the biggest band in the world, and Bono stuffed a deeper engagement with Africa into his cache of good intentions.

(debt, AIDS, trade, Africa) and the results-oriented political world (democracy, accountability, transparency in Africa). Thanks to Bono's unique ability to get political enemies to break bread together on the subject of poverty, DATA began winning respect and showing results.

All that helped prepare Bono for the most daunting challenge to his powers of persuasion: the Administration of George W. Bush. When Bush took office in 2001, development groups presumed that debt, AIDS and trade for Africa would be at the bottom of his agenda, largely because Bush said they would be. But Bono had forged too many productive odd pairings to simply give up. He knew the key to reaching Bush was religion. Born to a Protestant mother and a Catholic father, Bono describes his faith as "promiscuous." He quotes Scripture and counts meetings with Pope John Paul II and Billy Graham among the most significant of his life. "I try to live it rather than talk about it because there are enough secondhand-car salesmen for God," he says. "But I cannot escape my conviction that God is interested in the progress of mankind, individually and collectively."

Evangelicals in the White House and then National Security Adviser Condoleezza Rice helped persuade Bush to

LEFT: ERIC FEFERBERG—AFP/GETTY IMAGES; RIGHT: YURI GRIPAS—REUTERS

meet Bono. Bush began softening Bush by appealing to his religiosity, and also began to talk about debt relief and poverty eradication in hardheaded, national-interest terms. After 9/11, he and DATA lobbied for new policies. Africa is 40% Muslim, Bono argued, noting that it might be nice to make some friends there.

In 2003 the Bush Administration launched the President's Emergency Plan for AIDS Relief (PEPFAR) and the Millennium Challenge Corporation (MCC). In two years, PEPFAR has paid for antiretroviral drugs for 400,000 Africans with HIV, while the MCC aims to dispense foreign aid by rewarding countries for being accountable. Bono stood by the President when he unveiled the MCC. "These are more than baby steps," Bono recalls thinking, "but to get them to be strides we need more than applause or hisses from me. We need a movement."

One of the ways to spark a movement is to create a defining moment. "We've had 2005 in mind for quite a while," Bono says. As early as 2003, he and others had

in the past. To their surprise, they didn't have to do much pitching. Over beers with some friends from the Treasury Department, DATA executives actually heard the words "So, tell us why can't we do 100% debt cancellation?" There were details to iron out, and the Treasury guys insisted Bono not be told for a while (he is a poor secret keeper), but willingness proved 95% of the battle.

To cap it off, the G-8 would fall almost precisely on the 20th anniversary of Live Aid, and Bono wanted a concert to prove how far the movement had come. Geldof "didn't want to repeat himself," says Bono, but six weeks before the summit he hit upon the idea of staging free concerts in each G-8 country. After a frenzy of persuasion, cities were lined up, sponsors found and bands, many of which already had concerts scheduled for the day, were persuaded to divert from their itineraries and play for free.

Bono, meanwhile, launched a final burst of back-room politicking, greasing countless surreal encounters with people who had no business being in the same room together.

... **Nelson Mandela**   ... **former Treasury Secretary Paul O'Neill**   ... **Pope John Paul II**

FROM LEFT: FRANK MICELOTTA—GETTY IMAGES; SAURABH DAS—AP/WIDE WORLD; VATICAN/REUTERS

picked out a number of unrelated political events—a G-8 meeting that was to have as hosts British Prime Minister Tony Blair and Chancellor of the Exchequer Gordon Brown (dubbed by Bono the "John and Paul of global development"), a meeting of the World Trade Organization, a U.N. summit to review progress toward the Millennium Development Goals—all relevant to lifting people out of poverty. But they needed to be tied together and pitched as potentially world changing. "Politicians are performers of a kind, but they're not great at dramatizing a situation," says Bono. "These issues need tension, jeopardy and a sense of what-might-be to succeed. All of that is much more from our language than from theirs."

A tour de force of syndicalism followed. Several NGOs in the oft-backbiting development community put aside their differences and launched integrated awareness campaigns (Make Poverty History in Britain, the ONE Campaign in the U.S.) aimed at educating people about global poverty and registering millions of supporters online. Blair announced a G-8 agenda with a priority of getting $50 billion in aid and 100% debt cancellation, and DATA lobbied the White House to be an active partner, reminding it that Blair had stood by the Administration

Days before the summit, he visited 10 Downing Street and learned that the G-8's civil-servant negotiators, or "sherpas," who put deals into precise language, were feuding over how to pay for the proposed $50 billion aid package.

"We were having a beer," Blair told TIME, "and just decided we would talk to these people who'd done an incredible amount of work, to give them a sense of the importance of this." After introducing himself, Bono asked them to "please go that bit further," reminding them that "in 20 years, this week is one of the things you'll be most proud of in your lives." Says Blair: "These are all pretty hard-bitten people who have worked in international relations a long time, but they were very, very enthused by that spirit."

Just before the end of the summit—which was disrupted by the July 7 terrorist attacks in London—Bono dropped by President Bush's suite for a final nudge. "On so many issues it's difficult to know what God wants from us," Bono told Bush, "but on this issue, helping the desperately poor, we know God will bless it."

On July 8, the leaders agreed to cancel the debt of the 18 poorest African countries and to adopt the $50 billion aid package by 2010. And that's a fact. "Facts," Bono says, "are very beautiful." But only Bono can make them sing. ■

FROM RICHES TO RAGS

Imagine a kinder, humbler Microsoft—one designed to spend money, not make it. That's the kind of philanthropy Bill and Melinda Gates have invented. The story of a very risky venture

By Amanda Ripley/New Delhi, with Amanda Bower

"The man who dies rich dies disgraced."
—ANDREW CARNEGIE

AT LEAST ONCE A YEAR, BILL AND MELINDA GATES LIKE TO TAKE WHAT they call a "learning tour" of the places that civilization has largely forgotten. On Dec. 6 in India, on the most recent of such visits, they left the five-star Taj Mahal Hotel in New Delhi, to which they had flown on their private jet the night before, and took a 20-minute drive to a slum colony in an area called Meera Bagh. On the way, through rickshaw traffic jams and past lumbering cows, a local doctor briefed them on the slum's 9,000 residents and five health-care workers. Melinda listened intently with her eyebrows raised, as she almost always does, while Bill interrupted to ask the kinds of questions you would expect from a capitalist billionaire. "Who owns the land?" (The doctor wasn't sure; probably the government.) "How much do the health-care workers earn?" (Ten dollars a month.) "Is that a full-time job?" (No.)

SHOW AND TELL: In a building that is only half standing, the Gateses talk with Bangladeshi women about how they start businesses with small loans
Photographs for TIME by James Nachtwey—VII

Once they arrived, they strolled through the narrow alleys lined with staring children. Bill, in a black fleece pullover and khaki pants, stuck his hands in his pockets and squinted into the sunlight, not unlike a man walking down the fairway at Augusta. Several times they stopped to talk with families. In unit No. 774, they found Sushila and Suraj Naik, who live in the windowless space with their daughter Puja, 3, and a tiny new baby called Liza. The Naiks welcomed them, offering them the only seat in the unit—on the double bed that took up almost the entire room. The space was lit by a single bare lightbulb. Through an interpreter, the Naiks patiently answered all the Gateses' questions.

Sushila, dressed in a red sari, smiled broadly the whole time, showing improbably white teeth. Yes, her daughter Liza was born here in this room a month ago. Her husband is a carpenter. They pay $13 a month in rent. Melinda held Liza for a few minutes, and then she and Bill got up to go. "Very impressive," said Bill, using his default version of thank you. "*Namaste* [goodbye]," said Melinda, holding her palms together and bowing slightly.

After the Gateses returned to the hotel, I went back to Meera Bagh to talk to Sushila. She was giving her children a bath, but she stopped to play hostess to yet another foreign inquisitor. I asked Sushila whether she knew the names of the people who had visited that morning. She said that she did not but that they were very nice. I told her the man in the khaki pants was the richest man in the world. Sushila smiled and said it didn't matter that he was the richest. All foreigners were rich compared with her, she said.

There are many places the Gateses could go together for an adventure. That they chose to come to India and Bangladesh to sit on concrete floors and talk about tuberculosis and diarrhea sets them apart from most globe-trotting billionaires. But their relationship with the developing world is even more complicated than that. As they tour hospitals and huts, they seem to delight in these escapades, not just because they are intellectually captivated by the scientific challenge of treating the diseases of the poor but also because they are convinced that they are living through a historic inflection point when medical breakthroughs could save the lives of millions. They see the Bill & Melinda Gates Foundation not as a solution but as a catalyst for this progress: pumping resources and rigor into the fight just when scientists are inventing new tools that could change everything. "This is a magic time in terms of the momentum we can get going," Bill says later.

And beneath all those grand ambitions, there is another force at work: they get a kick out of sharing these pilgrimages as a couple, and they prefer it if people don't know who they are. "We're just people from the moon, as far as they know," says Bill. Later, they spend hours talking about everything they've seen. Says Melinda: "That's a huge side benefit. We love doing this together."

IN ITS SIX-YEAR EXISTENCE, THE GATES FOUNDATION HAS accomplished a fraction of what it aims to do. But already it has helped save at least 700,000 lives in poor countries through its investments in vaccinations. In the U.S., its library project has brought computers and Internet access to 11,000 libraries. And it has sponsored the biggest privately funded scholarship program in history, sending 9,048 high-achieving minority students to college. It is the

ON TOUR After flying all night from Seattle, the Gateses arrive in Dhaka, Bangladesh, to tour slums and meet grantees

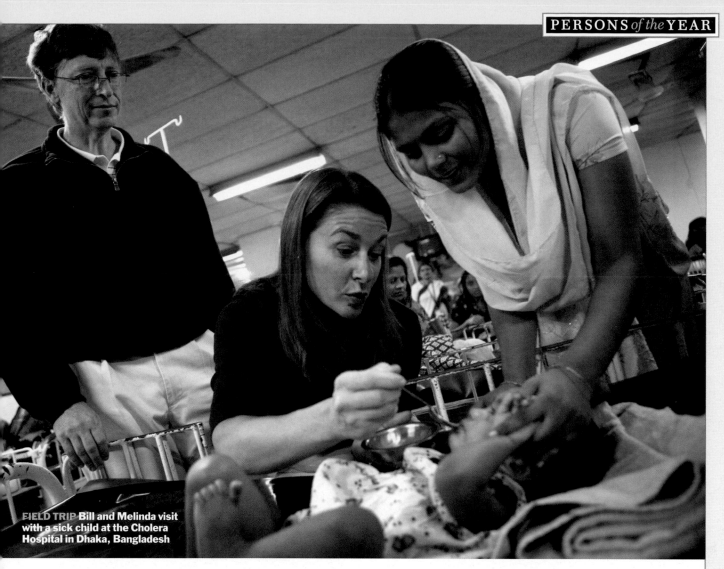

FIELD TRIP Bill and Melinda visit with a sick child at the Cholera Hospital in Dhaka, Bangladesh

largest foundation in the world, with an endowment of $29 billion. Each year it spends almost the same amount as the World Health Organization (WHO). In public health in particular, to which the foundation devotes 60% of its funds, "it's the most important organization in the world," says former President Jimmy Carter. The Carter Center, which has been working to eradicate guinea worm disease since 1986, received a pledge of $25 million from the foundation this year. "They know what they're doing," he declares.

But all that pales in comparison to what the foundation has done for the public imagination. For decades, the field of global health had languished, and there was a consensus that little could be done to change the fate of the poorest of the poor. Jim Kim, until recently director of WHO's department of HIV/AIDS, refers to that dark period as BGF (Before the Gates Foundation). Now, says Kim, "the Gates Foundation has made global health cool."

In 2003 President George W. Bush announced a five-year, $15 billion HIV/AIDS treatment and prevention initiative, the largest commitment ever by a single nation to an international health effort. "It would have been outlandish to even consider that the U.S. government would do something like that before," Kim says. This year European nations pledged an astonishing $4 billion over 10 years to immunize children in poor countries—dwarfing the Gateses' $1.5 billion contribution. "When the history of global health is written," says Dr. William Foege, a former head of the Centers for Disease Control and Prevention (CDC)

who now advises the foundation, "the tipping point will be two people: Bill and Melinda Gates."

BOTH GATESES GUARD THEIR PRIVACY CLOSELY, BARRING reporters from their plane and their home in Seattle. Melinda, in particular, has resisted the attention that comes with their wealth. For the first nine years of their marriage, she declined almost all media interviews. She quit her job at Microsoft after she had their first child in 1996. "I wanted to have some privacy in our community," she says. "When I took the kids to a preschool event, I could be like all the other moms." Only after their youngest child, Phoebe, turned 1 did Melinda begin to go public. "Bill and I both felt it was important that people know we're both behind the foundation," she says. And the more she traveled in the developing world, the harder it was to keep quiet. "I was very moved. I felt that I had a role to give some voice to the voiceless."

Their friends and the staff at the Gates Foundation go to great lengths to emphasize that Melinda and Bill are equals. "She is not a junior partner in any way, shape or form. Bill likes that," says Warren Buffett, a close friend (and the second richest man in the world, for those who are counting). Says Sylvia Mathews, the foundation's chief operating officer: "We joke and say Bill and Melinda have 2½ degrees: she has two; he has a half." (Melinda, 41, has a bachelor's degree in computer science and economics and a master's in business from Duke University. Bill, 50,

FACT FINDING **In a New Delhi slum, a mother waits for the translation of the Gateses' polite questions**

dropped out of Harvard at the end of his sophomore year to run Microsoft.)

Despite what anyone says, it's clear that the big decisions get made by Bill Gates. At a quarterly review of grants at the offices in Seattle, he sits at the head of the table, with Melinda on his left and his father on his right. Nervous staff members direct their presentations to him, not Melinda—who drinks a Snapple and seems like the most relaxed person in the room. Bill flings out questions in his trademark squeaky voice, with an expression on his face that suggests more curiosity than concern.

On their trips to the developing world, however, the dynamic changes. Talking to women in hovels about condom use, Bill sits with his hands in his lap, nodding robotically, while Melinda leans forward to ask questions and hold babies. When I ask whether there is a formal division of labor between the two, Bill demurs. "It's like saying, Who is raising our children?" When Melinda goes to Africa, she calls Bill to share her stories.

And when they travel together, they make each other laugh. "Take the arrival at the airport in Bangladesh," says Bill. Given that there was a string of terrorist bombings in the days before their arrival, the military was out in force. And the tarmac was festooned in decorations to welcome the Gateses—including, bizarrely, a massive oil portrait of each. "She saw the army," says Bill, laughing. "She said, 'Hey, there's an army out here.' And I said, 'Yeah, wait until you see the picture of you. It's not too good.' It was just gigantic! You know, Mao would have been so jealous!" Some couples have ballroom dancing. The Gateses have saving the world. And they like to do it the uncomfortable way, by looking straight into lives they know nothing about.

BACK IN SEATTLE, THOUGH, THE GATESES SHOW LESS PAtience. They run the foundation like a business. They are remarkably fluent in the science of public health ("I suspect Bill Gates knows more about the molecular biology of mosquitoes than 95% of the doctors in the world," says Kim). And both use the language of business to describe the human experience. "There is no better return on investment than saving the life of a newborn," Melinda told reporters at a November press conference. Melinda is in the foundation office about two days a month. Bill is still busy being chairman of Microsoft, but they are both in regular contact with the staff, and they each spend about 15 hours a week on foundation business.

It's easy to forget that Gates was considered a philanthropic deadbeat just over a decade ago. By 1992 he had given away more than $21 million, mostly to local charities and schools. But since he was worth $8 billion, the local papers were not impressed. Even his parents were concerned. Before Bill and Melinda were married in 1994, Mary Gates, his mother—a former teacher, lifelong volunteer and community activist—gave a letter to Melinda in which she stressed the great opportunities the two would have, as well as the responsibilities. "From those to whom much is given, much is expected," she wrote.

But Bill's plan was to wait 20 or 30 years, until he had retired, to create a foundation. "He was one of the busiest people in the world," says his father, Bill Sr., a prosperous lawyer and supporter of the United Way and University of Washington, who is known to everyone at the foundation as "Senior." "He didn't want to have another entity to worry about." But solicitations were pouring in—and piling up, unanswered. "Anybody who had an eye out for a dollar was mailing letters to the richest man in the country," his father says.

Bill Sr. was painfully aware of the complaints about his son's indifference. In 1994, not long after Mary died, as he was waiting in line to see a movie with Bill and Melinda, he volunteered to help them start answering the requests. His son agreed. "I was willing to start early because I had someone I trusted to carry it out," Bill says. So they set up the William H. Gates Foundation in Bill Sr.'s basement rec room. He used his home address, until the post office complained about the volume of mail.

At first, Bill and Melinda focused their international giving on population control and reproductive health. But soon they learned that better health leads to smaller populations. In 1998, Bill Sr. came across a progress report from the International AIDS Vaccine Initiative, a small nonprofit organization, based in New York City, working to speed the search for a vaccine. In the margins, he wrote a note to Bill and Melinda: "I don't know what we can do about this. But if this isn't what philanthropy is for, I don't know what is."

dowed the Bill & Melinda Gates Foundation with an initial $17 billion. They folded the old foundation into the new one and persuaded Bill Sr. to move out of his basement and into a real office. Patty Stonesifer, a former Microsoft executive who had been running the Gateses' library project, joined him to lead what was suddenly the biggest philanthropy in the country.

"When you write the check, you think, Hmm, that's a lot of zeros," Bill admitted to PEOPLE that year. But by then, he and Melinda had Jennifer, then 3, and Rory, just 7 months. And parenthood was changing them in ways they were just beginning to understand. "Melinda and I talked about the things we believed in for our own kids. You want them safe and healthy," he said at the time. The worst thing they could do for their kids, they decided, would be to leave them all their money. Bill had read a 1986 FORTUNE story about the perils of inherited wealth, and it confirmed what he had noticed at his élite private high school in Seattle. "The ones who were the wealthiest weren't the most motivated," he says. The bulk of his $46.5 billion fortune will go to the foundation, but he and Melinda have not decided how much to leave their children. "Our thinking will evolve," he says.

Once the Gateses committed to working on global health, the foundation began to grow much faster than anyone anticipated, Stonesifer recalls. Very soon, however, they realized that they could never do what they hoped to do

"I think you have to be very careful to only speak out about a few things. If you have some credibility, it only goes a small distance."

— BILL GATES

Bill sent back a one-word reply: "Agreed." And so the foundation issued its largest grant to date: $1.5 million.

Soon afterward, one of the foundation's advisers gave Bill a copy of a 1993 World Bank Development report. Today it reads like a blueprint for the Gates Foundation. Using just the kind of steely analysis that Bill loves, the 329-page document explained how many millions of people in poor countries die from diseases that already have cures. Then it listed the most cost-effective methods of preventing those deaths: from immunization to AIDS prevention to nutrition, all of which would become major investment areas for the foundation. Finally, he had found what every well-meaning billionaire wants: a formula to make a guaranteed difference. One weekend, Melinda and Bill pored over the report. "Very quickly, we came to the point that this was something we wanted to do," says Melinda.

And so, in 1999, the same year Bill became worth $100 billion (on paper) and one year into an epic antitrust suit brought against Microsoft by the U.S. government, they en-

because even their money was a drop in the bucket. Instead of downsizing their ambition, they decided they needed other organizations and countries to step up and make the foundation look puny.

So Bill, Melinda and Patty began to do things they had sworn they would never do. Although as a nonprofit they are forbidden to lobby for legislation, they are allowed to "educate." They opened an office in Washington and began meeting with politicians all over the world, including British Prime Minister Tony Blair, former German Chancellor Gerhard Schröder, French President Jacques Chirac and U.S. Secretary of State Condoleezza Rice.

And to rally more outside help, they started exploiting the media attention Bill inevitably attracts. In January, for example, the Gates Foundation gave $750 million, spread over 10 years, to the Global Alliance for Vaccines and Immunization (GAVI) to immunize children in poor countries. Norway pledged $290 million over five years. But every time he spoke to a reporter about his donation, Bill Gates

CRUNCHING NUMBERS Melinda
Gates confers with staff before giving
$84 million for newborn health care

mentioned Norway. This month Norway announced it would give close to $1 billion over 10 years. "When I'm speaking to the press, I'm thinking, Who are the people I should praise?" says the newly media-friendly Bill. In our interviews he repeatedly mentioned pharmaceutical company GlaxoSmithKline and, well, Norway.

The Gateses say GAVI is their smartest investment yet. This year, when five European nations backed them up with an unprecedented $4 billion over 10 years to fund GAVI's work, it was all about leverage. At the World Economic Forum in Switzerland, Bill Gates and his new ally, Bono, had tag-team meetings with Blair, Schröder and others, using the example of one as peer pressure for the other. Bill remembers once telling Bono he wasn't sure Schröder would come around. Bono was undeterred. "I tend to be a little more realistic," Bill says. "He's always saying, 'Yeah, we can do this!'"

So far, Bono has been more right than wrong, something that seems to amaze Bill, who is not easily impressed. If you're not talking to him at a very high level about science or business, you're wasting his time, and he lets you know it. (In our first interview, he didn't look at me for 15 minutes. Melinda fielded the soft questions he couldn't bear to handle, as she often does.) But Bono talks about global problems on a very high level, and one senses their friendship is one of the great surprises of Bill's life. "It's not about making himself look good," Bill says. "He really reads this stuff; he cares about the complexity."

In April the Gateses had U2 to lunch. "Bono thought it was important for us to get to know the other band members," Bill says. "They give him the license to spend time and credibility on this. This way I could say, 'Look, Bono is really, really having an impact. You should feel superproud about the leniency you're giving Bono to do this.'"

That night the Gateses went to their first U2 concert. The next night they went back to see the group again. They were stunned by the way Bono could move thousands of people at a rock concert to vow to make poverty history. Bono slept at their house, and the three of them stayed up until 3 a.m. scheming about the G-8 summit and listening to Bono's impressions of Martin Luther King Jr. and Bobby Kennedy.

EACH DAY, THE GATES FOUNDATION RECEIVES ABOUT 140 requests for aid. (It was a major sponsor of the TIME Global Health Summit 2005.) Until now, the foundation has focused on education, libraries, global health and Seattle-area initiatives. But it may soon add water, sanitation and hygiene or financial services for the poor to the portfolio. Bill says he would also like to learn more about the Middle East and Asia. And he claims he will continue to increase the amount of time he devotes to the foundation.

There is a real risk that billions of dollars from the Gateses, no matter how leveraged, will not be nearly enough to reverse the slip-sliding decline in health in poor countries. There is an equally great risk that they will waste billions of dollars trying. It may be decades before they know if they have made the right choices. Foege, the former CDC director, compares what is happening in science today to the Middle Ages. "When you could finally bring the architects, the builders and the artisans together, you could finally build a cathedral," he says. "But the artisans working on the cathedrals knew they would never live to see them. And you can't see any evidence that their work suffered because of that."

Perhaps one reason so many cathedrals got built in the Middle Ages is that it is easier to raise a great edifice when there is a benevolent potentate in charge—with a long view and obscene sums of money. Today we have Bill Gates, hands stuffed in his pockets, squinting up at the framework of his unfinished cathedral. ∎

I N T E R V I E W

"WE JUST GO OFF"

GREGORY HEISLER FOR TIME

THREE OF A KIND
They can discuss
quantum physics or
stand-up comedy

THAT'S HOW BONO DESCRIBES THE LATE-NIGHT SESSIONS HE AND THE Gateses have when they meet. In an interview with TIME's Josh Tyrangiel in Omaha, Neb., in December, the rapport between the rocker and the tech lords was easy and their curiosity about one another's worlds genuine.

TIME *When you first had Bono over for dinner, in 2002, were you aware of his celebrity or nervous about it?*
MELINDA GATES: We'd certainly never had a rock star to the house before, but the whole reason we got together is because we have this joint cause. *[To Bono]* I have to be honest, we kind of came a lot later to your music than other people.
BONO: It was fresh not to be seen as a celebrity but as a piece in the puzzle of how we communicate the jeopardy of all those lives—and the opportunity of helping if we can just agree on something. It was nice not to be asked how the *Achtung! Baby* sessions went in Berlin.
M.G.: The first U2 concert we went to was in Seattle quite a bit later, and when you came out onstage, our reaction was quite different from your other fans'. It was more like "Oh, my gosh, does he know that all these people are here watching him? Oh, I hope he's O.K."

TIME *Are you bigger music fans now?*
BILL GATES: I've always been a music fan. Paul [Allen, Microsoft's co-founder] played guitar and made sure I knew all the Jimi Hendrix songs. He's a real music nut. Not many people create a music museum. [Allen founded Seattle's Experience Music Project.]
B.: You couldn't not listen to music if

Paul Allen was your partner. So Jimi Hendrix helped form *[slipping into a monster-movie voice]* "the Brain of Bill!"
B.G.: Paul would always say, "Are you experienced?" And it would mean different things at different times.
B.: We can ask Melinda about that. *[Laughter]*

TIME *Maybe next year. All of you deal with quite serious scientific and political issues, but there must be an emotional toll. Who's more likely to get angry or frustrated by the situation?*
B.G.: World health is something where, when you first realize the situation, it's pretty stark and even a bit depressing—just the magnitude of the inequity. But the more you work on it, you see the improvements that are taking place—that decade by decade new medicines are getting there. Maybe not as fast as they should, but you see the trajectory.
M.G.: When you visit a new country, you think, Oh, my gosh, maybe this is the time that I'm going to go somewhere and feel like there's no hope. But I don't think we've ever been in a situation where there hasn't been some glimmer.
B.: I get angry all right—but at myself and our inability to tell the story, to get the news

out that this need not be a burden but instead an adventure. But that anger is much more than made up for by the nobility of these people and their entrepreneurial nature. And then you see what a new medicine can do. Three years ago, the idea that nearly half a million Africans would be on antiretrovirals paid for by the U.S.A. was absolutely preposterous. That more than repays the anger.

TIME *You all have high-profile, time-consuming day jobs. Do you draw clear lines between your day jobs and this stuff?*
B.: It's tricky if you're recording a vocal to get called out because there's a finance minister on the phone. It's hard explaining that to the rest of the band. I've got to be careful because music is what's given me the license, and I have to serve it. I have crossed that line and gone too far. I'm trying to figure this out as we speak. It's not easy. The thing you've really got to watch is that it's always a life-or-death issue, so you can play martyr. If somebody doesn't play Live 8, it's like, "You're killing Africans!" *[Laughter]*
M.G.: That didn't work very well?
B.: I didn't do that, but I thought about it.

TIME *Bono's an equal partner in his day job.* [To the Gateses] *Does anyone tell you, "Hey, can you come and mind the store, please?"*
M.G.: We definitely step back once a month and say, Did we as a couple spend time on the right issues, be it the foundation, Microsoft, our children? And if it ever gets where it feels like it's not the right balance, then we reshuffle.

TIME *When the subject turns away from poverty and global health, what do you guys all talk about together?*
B.: We just go off. If you hung out with us, it gets quite jazz. We're united by deep curiosity. So from stand-up comedy to quantum physics, there's nothing we don't cover. For me, that's what makes [good] company.
B.G.: The night after that concert where we stayed up till almost 3 a.m., we talked a lot about how history shapes things. Some of us were more optimistic about the future than others.
B.: That'd be me then. ∎

IT STRUCK THE GULF COAST, BUT IT WOUNDED A NATION

KATRINA

SWAMPED This picture of a flooded New Orleans was taken on Sept. 1, three days after Katrina made landfall. The city is built on land that is substantially lower than adjacent Lake Pontchartrain. When the levees that hold back the brackish lake waters failed, the city effectively became a part of the lake

Hurricane Katrina began as a natural disaster; human error transformed it into a national disgrace. First the storm battered towns along the Gulf Coast and flooded the streets of New Orleans. Then Americans watched, horror-struck, as more than 1 million people fled their homes, while tens of thousands were stranded without food, water or power in the swamped Crescent City, which descended into lawlessness even as local, state and federal agencies proved unable to aid its residents. The storm revealed economic and racial divisions too often overlooked in today's America. It exposed glaring deficiencies in the emergency-response system at all levels of government. It threatened the future of one of the nation's most historic and beloved cities, rocked George W. Bush's White House and challenged Americans' vision of themselves and their nation.

But hurricane season wasn't over yet: the kicker arrived in the form of Hurricanes Rita, Stan and Wilma.

PHIL COALE—AP/WIDE WORLD

LEVEE BREACH By the afternoon of Aug. 29, only hours after Katrina made landfall, streets on the city's east side are swamped and residents are in peril

ORDEAL IN NEW ORLEANS

Katrina breaches the Crescent City's levees, and as authorities dither and bicker, the historic city turns into a flooded, crippled wasteland

WHEN HE TOOK TO THE AIRWAVES ON SEPT. 28 TO ADvise his fellow New Orleanians to flee the city as Hurricane Katrina approached, Mayor C. Ray Nagin said just what was on everyone's mind: "We're facing the storm most of us have feared." Indeed, every resident of the historic city—the beloved home of Mardi Gras, jazz and Bourbon Street—knew that its very existence was founded on defiance of Mother Nature, for it was built on land snatched from the water.

New Orleans grew up on a rare strand of high ground along the Mississippi River delta, where much of the land lies at or below sea level. As its trade and population boomed in the 19th century, New Orleans found itself strapped for space. The solution the city adopted amounted to a gamble, a quality suited to a town famously devoted to fantasy and fun: earthen levees were thrown up along the shores of nearby Lake Pontchartrain and the Mississippi, allowing entire sections of the city to be built on land lying well below the two bodies of water. In the 20th century, a series of improvements was made to the levees; engineers claimed that they would be able to withstand a Category 3 hurricane. Small wonder Mayor Nagin was pleading with his constituents to leave the city: earlier that day, the National Hurricane Center in Miami had upgraded Katrina to a Category 5 storm.

Most New Orleanians—upwards of 80% of the city's 485,000 residents, as well as large numbers from its contiguous suburbs—heeded Nagin's call to evacuate. Indeed, the city and state of Louisiana managed to pull off a very

LOOMING This Aug. 27 satellite image shows Katrina moving toward New Orleans and the Mississippi coast

successful evacuation, given that there are a only a few northbound routes leading out of the city. But that left a glaring problem that would soon capture the attention of the world: the residents who did not leave town were those who did not own vehicles, or know a friend who owned one, or who were restricted from leaving by age, poverty or in-

ABOVE: RICK WILKING—REUTERS—CORBIS; LEFT, NASA

firmity. In short, as Hurricane Katrina drew a bead on the city, those residents left to face its wrath were disproportionately old, impoverished, ailing and black.

Landfall On the night of Sunday, Aug. 28, Katrina was hovering off the coasts of Louisiana and Mississippi, poised to strike. Then the storm seemed to give New Orleans a break: it veered slightly to the east. When the hurricane made landfall, about 6 in the morning of Aug. 29, it vented its main force against the Mississippi coastline, which took a terrible battering from high winds and a monster storm surge. In a semideserted New Orleans, the hurricane's high winds tore down trees and damaged buildings. But at first glance, the city seemed to have weathered the storm well. Americans watching on TV and listening to radio reports breathed a sigh of relief as the grand old town seemed to have once again defied fate.

But Katrina had grievously damaged the city, if subtly at first, attacking its weakest point, the levees. The Industrial Canal, which holds back the waters of Lake Pontchartrain from the Ninth Ward and St. Bernard Parish, two of the lowest-lying areas in the city, was breached around 8:14 a.m.; by 1 p.m. there was 8 ft. of water in the streets of the Ninth Ward. The levee along the 17th Street Canal was also breached, in the early afternoon; it gradually widened until, around midnight, a section as long as a football field ruptured. New Orleans was now filling up like a superbowl with brackish waters: the historic city had become a lagoon, an annex of Lake Pontchartrain. The breaches left 80% of the city submerged and as many as 80-100,000 residents stranded amid the floodwaters. As the temperature rose, most of the city was poached in a vile stew of chemicals, gasoline, oil spills and human waste.

For the first time ever, a major U.S. city was taken offline, closed down. Food and water and power and phones were gone; authority was all but absent—about one-sixth of the city's police officers failed to report for duty in the immediate days after the storm. In the vacuum of power, looting broke out, and wild rumors ran rampant. Some 25,000 people took refuge at the city's designated shelter for those unable to leave, the Superdome athletic arena. But even there the power was operating on generators, while food, fresh water and authority figures were scarce.

New Orleans, a city known both for its charm and its

"Half of Louisiana is under water, and the other half is under indictment." —Former Congressman Billy Tauzin

rot, not just from the termites consuming whole neighborhoods but from a corrupt police force, dissolving tax base, neglected infrastructure, rising poverty and a brutal murder rate, could hardly have been less equipped to cope with a catastrophe that everyone knew might one day appear. "Half of Louisiana is under water," former state lawmaker Billy Tauzin used to say, "and the other half is under indictment." Three of the top state emergency officials had been indicted in 2004 for mishandling disaster funds.

DAVE MARTIN—AP/WIDE WORLD

THE TREK David Keifer, his sister Molly and his son William brave the streets two days after Katrina hit

LOST Fires devour homes in the Garden District. The blazes were reportedly set by looters traveling by boat

The Rescuers New Orleans was now a filthy, fetid simulacrum of Venice: corpses floated through its flooded streets, uncollected, as rescue efforts bypassed them; emergency workers were too busy saving the living to attend to the dead. A bizarre flotilla of watercraft—Everglades airboats and Sea-Doos, rubber rafts and canoes—carried an ad hoc crew of rescuers from house to house.

Some of the rescuers represented emergency agencies; some were U.S. soldiers and sailors; some were volunteers from nearby states; some were New Orleanians—all were determined to save those stranded by the storm. As they floated through the swamped city, they could hear people pounding on roofs from the inside, trapped in attics as the waters rose; the lucky ones were able to cut holes with knives and axes to reach the open air.

Above, the skies were abuzz with helicopters, which plucked stranded survivors, one at a time, from the rooftops. "It was like a pickup game," Lieut. Commander Bill Howey, a Navy helicopter pilot, told TIME's Adam Pitluk. "You got three or four different types of Army helicopters, same for the Navy. Then there's Customs, Coast Guard, Marines, and then there are the news helicopters." The choppers airlifted the sick from around the city to the airport, which was converted into a field hospital, or to evacuation sites scattered on the outskirts of the city.

In the few hospitals left operating, doctors and nurses fought to keep people alive until rescue came. But as the agonizing days ticked by, no rescue arrived at the hospitals; at the city's nursing homes; at several points of high ground around the city, where survivors had fled for refuge; at the Superdome; or at the Ernest N. Morial Convention Center, pressed into service as a backup sanctuary for another 20,000 residents when the Superdome became overcrowded. Americans watched in disbelief as

their fellow citizens suffered travails more commonly seen in Third World nations. Everyone was waiting for the bugle to sound and the cavalry to arrive. But the bugle didn't sound the day after the storm, or the day after that, or the day after that. The cavalry, it seemed, wasn't coming.

The Authorities While New Orleans simmered and stewed in its own filth, government agencies fumbled the ball. The chain of errors began at city hall, continued to the Louisiana statehouse and ended up at the White House. Although New Orleans officials had known for decades that the city was a sitting duck for a major hurricane, emergency plans were vague and imprecise—and notably failed to take into account those unable to evacuate the city. The city did have a plan, of sorts: a week after the storm struck,

SAVED A Sea-Doo takes on precious cargo

THOMAS DWORZAK—MAGNUM PHOTOS FOR TIME

GARY CORONADO—PALM BEACH POST/ZUMA PRESS

MELISSA PHILLIP—HOUSTON CHRONICLE/WPN

AUG. 31: As National Guard troops look on, sunlight streams through two holes that Katrina's winds tore in the Superdome's roof when it hit New Orleans on Aug. 29

TWIN HEARTS OF DARKNESS

The events at two locations in New Orleans—the Superdome, home of the National Football League Saints, and the Ernest N. Morial Convention Center, an exhibition hall—summed up the disarray and confusion that marred the response to Katrina by emergency agencies at every level. Thousands of residents sought shelter from the floodwaters at the two sites, where conditions soon became horrific, although many of the initial reports of murders and rapes occurring within them proved erroneous.

As Katrina approached the city, Mayor C. Ray Nagin directed citizens unable to evacuate to head for the enormous Superdome; located on high ground, safe from floodwaters, it had previously served as a storm refuge. By the morning of Sept. 29, when Katrina made landfall, an estimated 20,000 New Orleanians had taken shelter within the building; they listened in awe as the hurricane's winds battered the building's roof and ripped two holes in it. The building's power went out in the first hours of that morning, plunging it into darkness until generators took over; for the rest of the week there was dim light, no fresh air, no working toilets in the building. Worse, there seemed to be no evacuation plan in place to remove the stranded: as the world watched on TV and listened on the radio, thousands of people waited in intolerable conditions for help, while FEMA officials and Louisiana authorities quarreled over who should be providing evacuation buses.

On Tuesday night, with the Superdome now housing 25,000 people, city officials directed citizens to use the Convention Center as a refuge. However, no plans were in place for using that facility as a sanctuary, and when some 25,000 residents gathered at the center, conditions soon mirrored those at the Superdome. Day after maddening day, the increasingly hungry, thirsty, restless, crowds at both facilities waited … and waited … to be evacuated.

When Dr. Greg Henderson, a pathologist now turned field medic, arrived at the Convention Center on Friday, he was the only doctor for 10,000 people. "They're stacking the dead on the second floor," he told TIME by phone. "People are having seizures

in the hallway." Henderson went in with New Orleans police, and when people saw him in scrubs, they surged at him from every side; he tried to tend the sickest and the babies first.

Later that day, assistance finally arrived: thousands of National Guard troops rolled into the city and began conducting an orderly bus evacuation of the Superdome; the evacuation of the Convention Center was mainly conducted on Saturday.

Sadly, Americans may long remember the frightening reports of crime and chaos at both buildings that were first broadcast in the heat of the crisis; many of these accounts of crime, gang rape and murder turned out to be founded in the hearsay that feeds urban myths. In fact, 10 bodies were found at the Superdome; of these, four were apparently brought in from the street and six were believed to have died within: four of natural causes, one of a drug overdose and one of a fall from a balcony that was an apparent suicide. Of four deaths known to have occurred inside the Convention Center, three were from natural causes and one was a homicide. Twenty bodies were found outside the building, but those deaths are not believed to have involved crimes. ∎

ERIC GAY—AP/WIDE WORLD

WAITING: A mother breaks down outside the crowded Convention Center

DISPLACED New Orleans evacuee Rochada Drummer takes a last look at the house she is leaving behind. Her two children are in the boat ahead

BERNARD WEIL—TORONTO STAR/ZUMA PRESS

Nagin summarized it for the *Wall Street Journal:* "Get people to higher ground and have the feds and the state airlift supplies to them." Most people did find their way to higher ground, but no supplies were finding their way to them.

Although New Orleans had received a $7 million federal grant in 2003 for a communications system that would connect all the region's first responders, the network failed soon after Katrina struck. For two critical days after the storm, Mayor Nagin—a former telecommunications executive elected in 2003 on a platform pledging to end the city's corruption—was cut off along with his emergency team, holed up in the Hyatt Regency Hotel, fending off

gangs of looters. It remains unclear why the mayor and his team chose not to use the city's Mobile Command Center—designed for just such a disaster—or join the other local officials at the emergency center in Baton Rouge.

Yet communication also broke down in a more crucial way: local, state and federal officials seemed unclear about the lines of their specific responsibilities. Governor Kathleen Blanco seemed to have unrealistic expectations as to the role the Federal Government would play, as her aides later confirmed. "She thought [the U.S. response] would be more omniscient and more omnipresent and omnipowerful than it turned out to be," said one.

In fact, the Federal Government's response to the storm was tardy, awkward and insufficient. The problems began with the Federal Emergency Management Agency (FEMA), which had been absorbed into the larger Department of Homeland Security after 9/11 and which had lost many experienced disaster specialists in the process. Its director, Michael Brown, was a political ally of President Bush's with few credentials for his position. The agency proved more a bottleneck than a lifeline during the first days after the storm, failing to marshal the buses needed to evacuate New Orleanians, failing to supply temporary housing for evacuees, failing at seeming-

DAVID J. PHILLIP—AP/WIDE WORLD; (2)

AIRBORNE Hundreds of stranded New Orleanians were rescued by helicopter. The U.S. Coast Guard was one federal agency that performed well in Katrina's aftermath

ly every turn. Brown himself seemed unfamiliar with the rudiments of his job.

Brown's superior, Homeland Security Secretary Michael Chertoff, seemed equally clueless about the unfolding catastrophe. On Sept. 1 he had to be told by an NPR commentator about the miserable conditions at the New Orleans Convention Center, an ongoing drama familiar to any American following the news from New Orleans. That same day, a furious, frustrated Nagin took to the airwaves to issue a "desperate SOS" for aid.

As for President George W. Bush, he seemed on top of events as Katrina approached the U.S. mainland, placing calls to both the mayor and the Governor. But in the first critical hours after the storm struck, he was busy making political appearances in Arizona and California. As he belatedly made plans to visit the stricken region late in the week, his aides resorted to putting together a videotape of news accounts of the tragedy in order to familiarize him with it. When he did arrive on the Gulf Coast on Sept. 2, the President congratulated the hapless Brown for his

AT SEA **President Bush joins Governor Blanco, Mayor Nagin and others to survey the flooding in New Orleans**

STOIC **Milvertha Hendricks, 84, waits for relief in the rain outside the Convention Center three days after Katrina hit**

work, declaring, "Brownie, you're doing a heck of a job." Ten days later, the FEMA director was quietly removed from his position. The President's image as a take-charge, efficient executive was seriously damaged; his approval rating plunged to an all-time low by late October.

The Aftermath Finally, on Friday, Sept. 2, after endless days of turmoil, the long-awaited bugle sounded: a huge convoy of National Guard vehicles and troops rolled into the city, and evacuation of the Superdome and Convention Center began. Leading the cavalry was one of the few authority figures to earn Americans' gratitude during the Katrina saga, Lieut. General Russel Honoré, a native of Louisiana. The take-charge Army officer was out in the streets with his troops, directing convoys and telling anx-

ious Guardsmen to keep their weapons down. Calling Honoré the "John Wayne dude," Mayor Nagin said, "He came off the doggone chopper, and he started cussing, and people started moving."

In the weeks that followed, New Orleans was slowly pumped out—although Hurricane Rita again sent floodwaters pouring through the levee breaches. By Oct. 2, well in advance of the Army Corps of Engineers' initial estimates, the city was mostly dry. But the Crescent City had suffered a grievous blow, and the job ahead seemed immense: the rubble-filled city's infrastructure would have to be rebuilt, along with its levees. And what was to be done about the low-lying districts ruined by the storm?

On Sept. 15, President Bush addressed the nation from Jackson Square in the eerily deserted city. Declaring that "there is no way to imagine America without New Orleans," he pledged a massive federal effort to rebuild the city. Commentators immediately compared the size and complexity of the plan with Franklin D. Roosevelt's New Deal—a striking analogy to apply to a conservative Republican President. The plan's price tag was variously estimated at $150 billion to $200 billion, a massive new budget line in an age of record federal deficits. The levees of New Orleans can be patched up, but the task of fixing the manifold problems so glaringly exposed by the storm—for the Crescent City, for Louisiana, for FEMA, for the White House and for all Americans—may be much more difficult. The road to recovery promised to be long, winding, confusing, contentious—and all that jazz. ∎

BIG JOB **On Sept. 15, President Bush pledged a massive federal program to rebuild New Orleans**

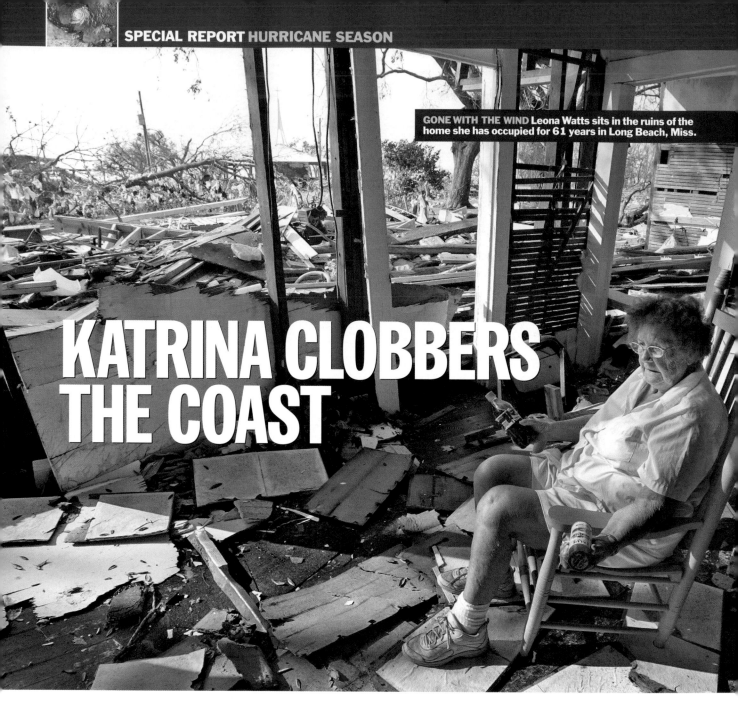

GONE WITH THE WIND Leona Watts sits in the ruins of the home she has occupied for 61 years in Long Beach, Miss.

KATRINA CLOBBERS THE COAST

Katrina works its worst damage on the coastline of Mississippi, where high winds and monster waves turn houses and buildings into flotsam

MARCIO JOSÉ SANCHEZ—AP/WIDE WORLD

BEFORE HURRICANE KATRINA STRUCK THE GULF COAST, the most devastating storm in recent U.S. history was Hurricane Andrew, which savaged Florida in 1992, killing 26 people, destroying 100,00 homes and causing up to $44 billion in damage. Yet veterans of Andrew who visited the Mississippi coast in the days after Katrina struck the region declared that the damage wrought by the 2005 hurricane was far greater than that of the earlier storm. Indeed, while the nation's attention was largely preoccupied by the plight of the citizens of New Orleans in the days after Katrina made landfall, the storm did far more damage to the Mississippi coast than it did to the Crescent City, which was largely spared the hurricane's high winds, succumbing instead to the breaches in its levees caused by the hurricane's mighty storm surge.

The story was very different in a series of towns spread along the Gulf Coast of Mississippi—Waveland, Bay St. Louis, Pass Christian, Long Beach, Gulfport, Biloxi, Ocean Springs—where historic mansions and expansive modern vacation homes mingle with tawdry motels, flashy casinos and the occasional shotgun shack. Here Katrina's winds did their worst, leveling buildings and uprooting grand old trees, while a storm surge sent waves as high as 20 ft. barreling ashore, shattering walls, flooding homes and lifting autos, trucks and railroad cars, then depositing them like so much crumpled-up litter on the newly flattened landscape. Stunned Gulf Coasters found themselves wandering through a world where a giant oil rig in drydock had been lifted and carried upstream, against the natural flow of a river, to smash into a bridge, and where enormous

JOHN BAZEMORE—AP/WIDE WORLD

RESCUE Terrence Gray, 28, guides Lovie May Allen to high ground from her flooded home in Gulfport, Miss.

what I went through," Shulz later remarked, "if I died right now and went to hell, I think I'd have it made."

There was heroism to match the horror. In Biloxi, Philip Bullard, 13, swam underwater from the attic of his home to locate a path through a submerged window that would lead his family to safety outside, then made seven trips back into the house, leading a family member out on each trip. In Gulfport, police maintenance worker Terrence Gray commandeered a boat he found on a railroad embankment, then fought steady 45-m.p.h. winds and high water to rescue more than 20 people trapped in the flooded streets of the Forest Heights neighborhood.

Colonel Joe Spraggins, director of the Gulfport Emergency Management Agency, said in the first hours after the storm, "Right now, downtown is like Nagasaki." Biloxi Mayor A.J. Holloway reached for another analogy: "This is our tsunami," he said. Meanwhile, in Gulfport, Mayor Brent Warr lost most of his official vehicles and ordered police officers to "borrow" residents' cars and gas supplies. He also ordered the police to break into a locked restaurant and "liberate" a stove to prepare meals for relief workers.

casino barges floating just offshore had been hefted off their moorings, carried ashore and plopped onto highways.

Local residents, many of whom had weathered severe storms before, found themselves overwhelmed by Katrina's power. Robert Barnes, a concrete finisher, took refuge from the rising floodwaters on his roof, only to find the waters rising so quickly that he was about to be swept away. He jumped into a nearby pine tree, lashed himself to its trunk with his belt and survived the waves. Brian Molere of Bay St. Louis, whose mother and grandmother had both lived through major storms, battled the waves for two hours, cradling his Chihuahua Rocky in his hands. His 80-year-old mother refused to leave the home she was in and was carried away by the waves. "I hope she went fast," Molere told TIME photographer John Chiasson.

In Biloxi, Kevin Shulz fought to save his family as the waves poured into the restored 19th century theater building where his family lived; as the group struggled to reach its roof, a wall collapsed, killing his mother-in-law. "After

"When you send your law enforcement out to steal things, you know you're in a different situation." —Gulfport, Miss., Mayor Brent Warr

"When you send your law enforcement out to steal things, you know you're in a different situation," he said.

By late October, the estimate of Katrina's damage in Mississippi alone totaled $30 billion; the death count in the state was 228. Residents vowed to restore their beautiful and historic coastline—and to stop betting against the house and put the state's casinos on solid ground rather than on floating dockside barges. ■

GREG RUFFING—REDUX

ROOM IN THE INN Left homeless, this mother and her two sons hole up in a battered motel in Bay St. Louis, Miss.

RISKY Benny Salas rides his bike along a pier in Galveston, Texas, on Sept. 23, as Rita's high waves crash around him

KATRINA'S KILLER COUSINS

Even as the Gulf Coast was reeling from Katrina, Hurricane Rita barreled into the region, and then hurricanes Stan and Wilma wreaked more havoc

O N SEPT. 18, EVEN AS AMERICANS WERE DEALING WITH the bitter fallout from Hurricane Katrina—and as some 1.3 million evacuees were trying to get adjusted to new lives in strange surroundings—a fresh tropical storm began brewing in the Caribbean. Within days, the system, dubbed Rita, had become a howling monster: the National Hurricane Center classified it as a Category 5 storm. Rita's 175 m.p.h. winds were every bit as powerful as those of Katrina at its height—and the storm was setting a course straight for the Florida Keys. Floridians, who had endured a quadruple drubbing in 2004 courtesy of Hurricanes Charley, Frances, Ivan and Jeanne, braced for the worst, and Governor Jeb Bush ordered the Keys evacuated. But Rita blew past the island chain on Sept. 20, sparing the southernmost part of the continental U.S. Then, setting a course that seemed almost malicious, the storm followed the general path of Katrina and headed toward the coasts of eastern Texas and western Louisiana.

As Rita approached, local, state and federal emergency agencies vowed they would not repeat the mistakes that had turned Katrina into a political and social calamity as well as a natural catastrophe. The first lesson was clear: the problems had begun with the failure to evacuate all citizens out of harm's way. So Governors Rick Perry of

JAM As Rita drew near and residents fled the city, Interstate 45 leading north out of Houston became a long parking lot

Texas and Kathleen Blanco of Louisiana issued mandatory evacuation orders for cities along the Gulf Coast, including Galveston, the Texas Gulf town devastated in 1900 by a hurricane that killed at least 8,000 people—the deadliest natural disaster in U.S. history.

In New Orleans, Mayor Ray Nagin had been encouraging residents to return to certain neighborhoods; now he

JIM MAHONEY—DALLAS MORNING NEWS

HIGHWAY TRAGEDY A bus evacuating residents from a Houston nursing home exploded on Sept. 23, killing 23

reversed himself and issued a mandatory evacuation order. Meanwhile, buses were ready and waiting to help get citizens out of town, while a new $4.5 million system employing military satellite technology went online, in hopes of averting the sort of communications breakdowns that had hampered an effective response to Katrina. At the federal level, FEMA dispatched more than 1,000 medical and rescue personnel to Texas, while President George W. Bush flew to the headquarters of the U.S. Northern Command in Colorado to monitor the progress of the storm.

In Texas, some 2.5 million people who had absorbed

"[Being tied up in traffic for hours] sure beats being plucked off a roof by a helicopter." —Texas Governor Rick Perry

Katrina's lesson headed north; Houston Mayor Bill White, whose city is the fourth largest in the nation, described the exodus as the largest mass evacuation in U.S. history. It may have been the slowest, as well: on Sept. 23, traffic was crawling along Interstate 45, the main route out of Houston to the north. In a glaring example of bureaucratic sloth, it took hours for state officials to convert the empty southbound lanes of I-45 into northbound lanes. A defensive Governor Perry pointed out that being stuck in traffic for hours, while no picnic, "sure beats being plucked off a roof by a helicopter." Meanwhile, as if to emphasize the manifold perils of hurricane season, a bus carrying residents of a nursing home in the city exploded on the highway, killing 23 passengers.

As Rita approached shore, its winds diminished and it was downgraded to a Category 3 storm. The hurricane made landfall not far from Sabine Pass along the Texas-Louisiana border on Saturday morning, Sept. 24, at about 3:30, sparing major cities a direct hit. But even a glancing blow from Rita's 120-m.p.h. winds and storm surge wreaked havoc in Galveston; many Americans were glued to their TV sets on Friday night, watching fire fighters battle flames and flying embers from a blaze that leveled three downtown buildings in the city.

Rita's assault was powerful, but its impact did not be-

gin to match that of Katrina. The storm worked its worst damage along the shores of Texas and Louisiana, flooding the streets of bayou towns and trashing homes and buildings. Although Rita did not strike New Orleans directly, its storm surge overtopped the city's hastily patched-up levees, and the streets of the Ninth Ward filled up with floodwaters once again, though the flood caused little additional damage and set back the pumping out of New Orleans by only three or four days. Rita's final death toll was more than 100, and damages were estimated at $6 billion.

More was to come: two weeks after Rita, another killer storm, Hurricane Stan, struck Central America, killing as many as 1,500 as its heavy rains led to mudslides. In late October Hurricane Wilma damaged tourist haunts in Mexico's Yucatan Peninsula, then hit lower Florida with floods and high winds. Coupled with the four storms that struck Florida in 2004, the hurricane season of 2005 served notice that an age of monster storms was upon us, and that shorelines all along the Gulf Coast were the front lines in a new war of man against the elements. ∎

BRENNAN WINSLEY—AP/WIDE WORLD

HURRICANE STAN STRIKES GUATEMALA

On Tuesday, Oct. 4, Hurricane Stan made landfall in Central America. The big storm proved a killer, although its modus operandi was different from that of Rita and Katrina: Stan's torrential rainstorms spawned huge mudslides in the highlands regions of Guatemala that engulfed entire villages. In the village of Panabaj alone, some 700 bodies were thought to be buried in the muck. Some villagers decided not to rebuild, effectively turning their former communities into mass graves. Throughout Central America, Stan left hundreds of thousands of people homeless and an estimated 1,500 dead.

MOISES CASTILLO—AP/WIDE WORLD

DOWNHILL At top, an overhead view of the crater left by a mudslide; above, the swamped village of Itzapa

DON CRAVENS—TIME LIFE PICTURES

A BUS RIDE INTO HISTORY

Few obituaries failed to note the signal ironies of Rosa Parks' life: this was a woman who moved a nation by sitting still, who stood tallest when sitting down. When, at age 42, the seamstress and veteran activist refused a Montgomery, Ala., bus driver's demand to yield her seat in the front of the segregated vehicle to a white man, she helped ignite a second American revolution, the civil rights movement, that struggled to achieve the Founders' deferred dream of inalienable rights for all. "I wasn't tired," she replied to reports that she was too exhausted to move on that historic day in 1955, "I was just tired of giving in." When Parks died on Oct. 24, at age 92, she was hailed as one of America's greatest citizens. As former U.S. poet laureate Rita Dove once wrote: "How she sat there,/ the time right inside a place/ so wrong it was ready."

Alberto Gonzales

WHEN *TIME* COMPILED A LIST OF THE 25 MOST INFLU-
ential Hispanics in the U.S. in 2005, there was little
doubt as to whose face would lead the procession:
in February, President George W. Bush appointed Alberto
Gonzales as the first Hispanic Attorney General in the nation's history. There's a certain symmetry at work here: in
1994, Bush persuaded Gonzales to leave a lucrative law
practice in Houston to be the new Texas Governor's general counsel, then Bush appointed Gonzales to the Texas
Supreme Court in 1999. When Bush moved on to higher
office, so did Gonzales: Bush brought the quiet, up-by-his-
bootstraps lawyer—who grew up in Houston in a home
boasting neither hot water nor a telephone—to Washington to serve as the White House counsel in his first term.

The post proved a hot seat for Gonzales: he defended the
Administration's refusal to release information about its
dealings with energy-industry execs; he helped craft the
controversial Patriot Act, which expanded federal power
in the name of fighting terrorism; he oversaw the selection
of Bush's very conservative judicial nominees. Most significantly, after 9/11 he was centrally involved in the meetings
and memos that set controversial guidelines for the treatment of suspected terrorists picked up overseas—leading to
a closer-than-expected Senate confirmation vote for his current post. Still in midcareer at age 50, Alberto Gonzales
may be an influential American for decades to come. ■

John Roberts

THROUGH THE FIRST MONTHS OF 2005, ALL Washington was gearing up for a monster battle over the anticipated first Supreme Court vacancy in 11 years. Yet after President George W. Bush named federal appeals-court Judge John Roberts as his choice to fill Justice Sandra Day O'Connor's seat following her July resignation, the city watched its political generals put their guns back into their holsters.

Slam dunk! Roberts had crafted a bulletproof résumé for the highest bench in the land. Born in Buffalo, N.Y., but raised in Long Beach, Ind., a small heartland town, he graduated from Harvard summa cum laude in three years, then was managing editor of the *Harvard Law Review.* He clerked for Justice William Rehnquist, worked in the Reagan and first Bush administrations and spent 14 years in private law practice in the capital. Bush appointed him to the Circuit Court of Appeals for the District of Columbia in 2003. Associates called him whip-smart, a brilliant litigator and, while conservative, far from an ideologue.

In his first round of private interviews with Senators, Roberts described himself again and again as "modest"—a deliberate word choice that liberals would read as suggesting he wouldn't overturn previous court decisions on issues like abortion and that conservatives would read as reassurance that he wouldn't be setting social policies from the bench. Roberts met with Senate minority leader Harry Reid, who praised the work Roberts had done for the environment in Reid's home state of Nevada. Roberts met with Senator Edward Kennedy and emerged not only with his hide intact but also with a gift map of Ireland in hand: turns out their ancestors lived only miles apart in the Old Country. Roberts met with such a warm welcome, in fact, that when Rehnquist died on Sept. 3 and Bush named Roberts to take his seat as Chief Justice, no one blinked an eye. Although five Democrats on the Judiciary Committee and 22 in the Senate voted against him, their opposition seemed pro forma. The youngest Chief Justice since John Marshall, Roberts, 50, may have many years to put his stamp on the court. Presidents come and go: Bush is No. 43. But Chief Justices just keep going: Roberts is No. 17. ■

Patrick Fitzgerald

ON OCT. 28, PATRICK FITZGERALD, THE SPECIAL PROSE-cutor investigating the leaking of CIA officer Valerie Plame's identity, announced the indictment of White House aide I. Lewis (Scooter) Libby in the case. Fitzger-ald, 44, spoke for an hour, almost entirely without notes, laying out a convincing case for his actions. His rigorous, dispassionate arguments injected a much needed sense of clarity and gravitas into a story that had been thoroughly politicized by polemicists on both the left and right. With his masterly presentation, the lawman served notice that there was at least one impartial mind on the scene.

The son of Irish immigrants, Fitzgerald grew up in Brooklyn, N.Y.; his bright mind and hard-working ways took him through Amherst College and Harvard Law School. In his 13 years as a prosecutor in the Southern Dis-trict of New York and four years as U.S. Attorney in Chica-go, Fitzgerald put away Mafia members, Islamic terrorists and drug kingpins, eventually becoming the nation's top

terrorism prosecutor. He put the blind Egyptian cleric Sheik Omar Abdel-Rahman behind bars after the 1993 World Trade Center bombing, then argued successfully to have him imprisoned in isolation. After the 1998 bombings of U.S. embassies in Kenya and Tanzania, Fitzgerald im-mersed himself in the case, learning about Islam and pick-ing up some Arabic in the process. His efforts resulted in terms of life imprisonment for four defendants.

Now based in Chicago, Fitzgerald is prosecuting former Illinois Governor George Ryan, a Republican, for corrup-tion; has pursued city workers for allegedly running a kick-back scheme; and has convicted a crony of Democratic Mayor Richard Daley's for using a sham minority firm to get millions in public money. "Do I have zeal? Yes. I don't pre-tend I don't," the no-nonsense Fitzgerald told the Wash-ington *Post* in 2005. "If you're not zealous, you shouldn't have the job." Single and childless, frequently working 100-hour weeks, Fitzgerald has the zeal—and the job. ∎

Ashley Smith

SHE IS ONLY 26, BUT THE GAZE IN ASHLEY SMITH'S EYES suggests wisdom beyond her years, acquired hard. The Duluth, Ga., waitress needed all the wisdom she could summon when she found herself cast in a taut two-person drama that ended in a moment of redemptive grace.

Smith thought she'd overcome a history of minor brushes with the law when she married carpenter Daniel Smith, then had a baby daughter, Paige. But after her husband was killed in a knife fight as she watched, Smith compiled a rap sheet for drunken driving, assault and probation violation and finally put in several months in a drug-rehab clinic.

Ashley Smith had been around: maybe that's why she refused to panic when an escaped prisoner and subject of a massive manhunt, Brian Nichols, followed her home from a 2 a.m. cigarette run on March 12, forced his way into her apartment and tied her up in the bathtub. Improbably, she

reasoned with the fugitive. Commiserating with him and baring her own wounds, she explained how a recent turn to Christianity had brought peace to her troubled life.

Nichols, 33, was desperate: in his flight, the defendant in a rape trial had killed four people in the prior 24 hours. But Smith spoke calmly to Nichols and persuaded him to untie her; she showed him pictures of Paige, 5, who was in an aunt's custody. She read to him from a Christian self-help book and urged him to surrender, helped him move his stolen truck, made him pancakes. Trust grew between them over seven hours; finally, Nichols allowed Smith to leave to visit Paige; she quickly called 911, and Nichols was arrested without incident. "She could relate," Smith's aunt said later. "I don't know think a socialite or a squeaky-clean could have done that." Nichols called her by another name, Smith recalled: he told her she was an angel. ■

THE LEAK

THE COURT

THE CONGRESS

THE AGENDA

THE STORM

THE WAR

SECOND-TERM PERFECT STORM

One year after winning re-election, President
George W. Bush confronts a sea of troubles

RICHARD NIXON HAD THE WATERGATE AFFAIR. RONALD
Reagan had the Iran-*contra* affair. Bill Clinton had
an adulterous affair and the impeachment mess that
resulted. Recent two-term U.S. Presidents have often found themselves struggling in Round 2. Yet it was still
surprising to see George W. Bush's crack West Wing operation experience a meltdown that hit bottom in a single
week at the end of October, as woes in all three branches of
the government united to create a perfect storm that left
the President's approval rating in free-fall.

The recipe for Bush's dilemma? On Oct. 28, I. Lewis
(Scooter) Libby, chief of staff to Vice President Dick Cheney,
was indicted by a special prosecutor in a case that high-
lighted the Administration's questionable rationale for the
U.S. intervention in Iraq. That mission, in which 159,000
U.S. troops in Iraq were bogged down fighting a many-
headed insurgency, reached a milestone the same week,
when the death toll of U.S. soldiers passed 2,000. When respected Pennslyvania Democrat Rep. John Murtha called
in November for a rapid withdrawal of U.S. troops, polls
showed many Americans agreed with him.

On Oct. 27, the day before Libby was indicted, White
House counsel Harriet Miers, Bush's nominee to replace
retiring Justice Sandra Day O'Connor on the Supreme
Court, withdrew her name after meeting opposition from
the right wing of Bush's own party. In choosing Miers,
widely viewed as unqualified for the job, the President
was also charged with cronyism, only six weeks after his ap-
pointee Michael Brown, the hapless, résumé-challenged
head of the Federal Emergency Management Agency, was
removed after fumbling the response to Hurricane Katrina.

Bush's party was also in trouble on Capitol Hill, where
House majority leader Tom DeLay stepped down from his
position to fight indictments on charges of money laundering, while Senate majority leader Bill Frist was under
investigation for possible illegal stock transactions.

On the Monday morning after his week from hell, the
President began to rebound, naming conservative federal
judge Samuel Alito as his new nominee for the Supreme
Court, to cheers from his Republican base. A December
White House offensive touting Bush's plans for victory in
Iraq, paired with good news on the economy, got his approval rating moving upward again. But the aura of invin-
cibility that once surrounded Bush's White House had dis-
solved; his second-term honeymoon was over. ▪

RIGHT: CHARLES DHARAPAK—AP/WIDE WORLD. LEFT, FROM TOP: RICHARD A. BLOOM—CORBIS; YURI GRIPAS—REUTERS; CHARLES DHARAPAK—AP/WIDE WORLD; STEVE NESIUS—AP/WIDE WORLD;
ERIC GAY—AP/WIDE WORLD; WATHIQ KHUZAIE—GETTY IMAGES. INSET AT TOP: ALEX WONG—GETTY IMAGES

FALLOUT New York *Times* reporter Judith Miller, above, served time in jail for refusing to name her source to a grand jury. Top White House adviser Karl Rove, right, remains a subject of investigation; Lewis Libby, left was indicted and resigned

THE LEAK

AN INDICTMENT AT THE WHITE HOUSE

For months, special prosecutor Patrick Fitzgerald's investigation into the leaking of the identity of covert CIA officer Valerie Plame seemed to be one of those bewildering inside-the-Beltway sagas that keep bloggers busy but try the patience of ordinary citizens. That changed on Oct. 28, when Vice President Dick Cheney's chief of staff, I. Lewis (Scooter) Libby, was indicted on charges of lying to a federal grand jury investigating the matter and immediately resigned his post. Americans began paying heed, for the case not only involved possible deceit in the White House but also touched upon the struggle between the Bush Administration and the intelligence community as they weighed the merits of the case for the U.S. intervention in Iraq, even as it raised questions about the role and rights of a free press in a democracy.

The story began in 2003, when Plame's husband, former U.S. diplomat Joseph Wilson, emerged as a well-credentialed critic of the Administration's case for the war. On July 6, only four months after U.S. troops invaded Iraq, Wilson wrote in an op-ed piece in the New York *Times* that "intelligence related to Iraq's nuclear weapons program was twisted to exaggerate the Iraqi threat." It was the most damaging charge that had yet emerged against the Administration's handling of prewar intelligence. Wilson explained that CIA officials recruited him to help them answer questions raised by Cheney's office about an intelligence report documenting the attempted sale by Niger to Iraq of uranium yellowcake, a substance used to create nuclear arms. The officials asked Wilson to travel to Niger in February 2002 "to check out the story," he said. His article suggested that when he failed to come up with the answers the

White House wanted, it ignored his findings, since President Bush later claimed in his January 2003 State of the Union message that, per British intelligence, Iraq had recently sought uranium from Africa.

Eight days after Wilson's piece ran, Plame's identity as a CIA operative was leaked in a column by conservative columnist Robert Novak, most likely in an attempt to punish Wilson by invalidating his credibility. All hell soon broke loose at the CIA; under a 1982 law, it is a federal crime to reveal the identity of a covert U.S. operative. The agency's lawyers launched an internal probe of the leak, and within months the Justice Department opened a

CATALYSTS: VALERIE PLAME AND JOSEPH WILSON
Joseph Wilson is a career U.S. foreign service officer and Africa expert who was called a hero by President George H.W. Bush after he served as chargé d'affaires in Baghdad during the run-up to the war with Iraq in 1991. He has become a vocal critic of the current war in Iraq. His wife Valerie Plame had worked undercover for the CIA over the course of two decades, most recently as an officer concerned with nuclear proliferation

CAROL JOYNT—GETTY IMAGES

CLOCKWISE FROM LEFT: RICHARD A. BLOOM—CORBIS; GERALD HERBERT—AP/WIDE WORLD; BROOKS KRAFT—CORBIS

criminal investigation. Fitzgerald, 44, was named special prosecutor *(see p. 44)* and quickly began hearing witnesses.

That, according to the indictment, is when Libby began to spin an intricate—and criminal—web of lies about his role in the leak. Although Libby declared under oath that he first heard about Plame's identity from reporters and passed it on to others as mere gossip, the indictment offers considerable evidence that it was the other way around—that Libby told two reporters, Judith Miller of the New York *Times* and Matthew Cooper of TIME, about Plame's work for the CIA and that he lied to investigators about one of those conversations and confected a third out of whole cloth. The truth may come out if Libby stands trial.

The indictment did not affect Cheney but left the President's longtime alter ego, political adviser Karl Rove—suspected by many to be involved in the affair—still under investigation. In November Fitzgerald impaneled a second grand jury, and he has questioned two more reporters about the leak: Bob Woodward of the Washington *Post* (who has revealed that Plame's name was given to him in 2003 by a source he refuses to identify publicly but did name in his deposition) and TIME reporter Viveca Novak, who also cooperated with Fitzgerald. As this book goes to press, the story of the leak seems far from resolved. ∎

CHRIS USHER FOR TIME

WHY THINGS AREN'T LOOKING UP FOR BILL FRIST
It was a tough year for Senate majority leader Bill Frist, who hopes to run for the presidency in 2008. After issuing an ill-informed long-distance diagnosis in the Terri Schiavo affair, the physician was outmaneuvered by moderates in his own party in a flap over judicial nominees. On Sept. 23 the Justice Department began investigating his possible violations of insider trading laws, probing whether he ordered the manager of his blind trust to dump his shares in a large health company founded by his family just days before the share price peaked and a month before poor earnings sent it plummeting. Frist declared his innocence and promised to cooperate with the probe

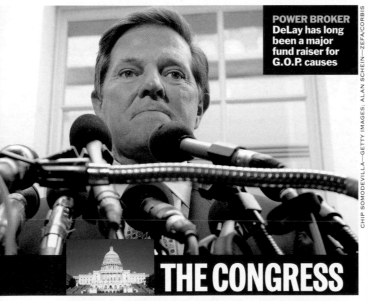

POWER BROKER
DeLay has long been a major fund raiser for G.O.P. causes

CHIP SOMODEVILLA—GETTY IMAGES; ALAN SCHEIN—ZEFA/CORBIS

THE CONGRESS

DELAY'S DILEMMA

WHEN HOUSE MAJORITY LEADER TOM DELAY GOT THE news on Sept. 28 that he had been indicted along with two political associates by a Texas grand jury for conspiring to funnel $155,000 in illegal corporate campaign contributions into legislative races in the state, his first words were, "Let's go fight." The combative Congressman, long known as "the Hammer," called his accuser, Travis County district attorney Ronnie Earle, "a partisan fanatic" who had engaged in his own conspiracy "with the Democratic leadership here in Washington."

The charges against DeLay are fairly simple. During the 2002 elections, a committee he founded to support conservative politicians—Texans for a Republican Majority, or TRMPAC—allegedly accepted $155,000 in corporate donations, then included that sum in a check for $190,000 to the Republican National Committee, which in turn routed a similar amount to seven Texas legislative candidates. Using corporate funds for state election purposes is illegal in Texas. DeLay's lawyers say the transactions were separate and that the PAC accepted money from both individuals and corporations. The funds helped produce a G.O.P. majority in the Texas legislature, which then redrew U.S. congressional district lines, helping add five more Republicans to the state's congressional delegation in Washington. G.O.P. caucus rules require that DeLay, 58, majority leader since 2003, give up his post while fighting the charges.

In November DeLay's lawyers successfully argued that a Texas judge identified with Democratic candidates should be removed from the case. On Dec. 5 the new judge dismissed a conspiracy charge, the least serious of the three, but let stand the charges of money laundering. As this book went to press, DeLay was pressing for a January start to his trial, in hopes of regaining his House post.

A separate federal investigation into the spreading scandal around disgraced lobbyist Jack Abramoff, long a close DeLay associate, had also begun lapping at the edges of the former majority leader's inner circle. Abramoff faces charges of bilking his clients, Indian tribes that own casinos, out of $66 million. His former partner (and DeLay's former press secretary), Michael Scanlon, pleaded guilty on Nov. 21 to conspiring to bribe a member of Congress and agreed to return more than $19 million in fees to his former Native American clients. Scanlon is cooperating with prosecutors in the Abramoff probe.

House Republicans were staggered anew on Nov. 28, when eight-term California Rep. Randy (Duke) Cunningham announced he would plead guilty to charges of accepting $2.4 million in bribes, mostly from military contractors. With a switch of only 15 seats required to end its House majority in the fall 2006 elections, the Grand Old Party can ill afford further damage to its reputation. ∎

RUTH BADER GINSBURG   DAVID SOUTER   CLARENCE THOMAS   STEPHEN G. BREYER

ANTONIN SCALIA   JOHN PAUL STEVENS   WILLIAM H. REHNQUIST   SANDRA DAY O'CONNOR   ANTHONY KENNEDY

THE REHNQUIST COURT
The death of the Chief Justice and resignation of O'Connor put the balance of conservatives and liberals on the court into play

THE COURT

ON THE BENCH, A TALE OF TWO SEATS

FOR MONTHS IF NOT YEARS, PARTISANS ON THE RIGHT and the left, in Washington and around the nation, have been gearing up for a massive fight over the next vacancy on the U.S. Supreme Court. The anticipation had a certain ghoulish aspect, for most observers believed that the vacant seat would be that of Chief Justice William Rehnquist, 80, who had been battling thyroid cancer for some time. But no one could have anticipated the unusual series of events that rocked the court in 2005, when not one but two seats came open, and not two but three nominees were advanced to fill them.

On June 30, White House counsel Harriet Miers took a call from Pamela Talkin, head marshal of the court, advising her that a sealed letter from a Justice would arrive at the White House the next day. But when it arrived, the letter did not concern the Chief Justice; it was a resignation notice from Justice Sandra Day O'Connor, the first woman Justice in history, who was appointed by President Ronald Reagan in 1981. That was big news, for O'Connor, 75, has for years been a critical swing vote on a court that is often divided 5 to 4 on such major issues as abortion, affirmative action and church-state relations. Her resignation electrified activist groups, particularly conservative and Christian organizations determined to ensure President George W. Bush didn't offer up yet another Republican nominee—like David Souter, Anthony Kennedy or for that matter O'Connor herself—whose votes are not consistently conservative. They demanded Bush uphold his campaign promise to appoint a Justice in the mold of Antonin Scalia

and Clarence Thomas, the anchors of the court's right wing.

The President's choice, announced on July 19, was John Roberts, a conservative judge and product of Harvard Law School with impeccable bearing and credentials (*see* p. 27). Yet even as Roberts was preparing for his confirmation hearings in the U.S. Senate, the capital was surprised again: on Sept. 3 Rehnquist died. The President quickly nominated Roberts to replace the Chief Justice and said that he would not declare his choice for O'Connor's seat until after the Roberts hearings were over. Justice O'Connor agreed to serve until her successor was in place.

NEW FACE, OLD FACE John Roberts is sworn in as the nation's 17th Chief Justice by the court's senior member, Justice John Paul Stevens, 85

Roberts sailed through the Senate hearings with relative ease, although he frustrated many Democrats with his coy demeanor and refusal to predict how he would vote on key issues. But Roberts' way was smoothed by the simple fact that he was a conservative replacing another conservative, Rehnquist. Democrats chose not to mount serious opposition to his candidacy, preferring to hold their fire until Bush announced his nominee for O'Connor's critical swing seat. The nomination of Roberts was approved 13 to 5 by the Senate Judiciary Committee and passed the entire body on a 78-to-22 vote. He was sworn in on Sept. 29.

A third surprise soon followed. On Oct. 3, Bush named his choice to fill O'Connor's seat: Harriet Miers. The news came as a bombshell, for Miers had appeared on none of the short lists circulating in the capital; she was far better known as a longtime Bush loyalist than as a student of the law. The Miers nomination ran into immediate trouble. Democrats attacked her relatively slim résumé and said her only qualification for the high court was that she was a political crony of the President's.

Surprisingly, the harshest attacks on Miers came from the right: conservative groups were appalled that Miers was not another Scalia, a brilliant scholar and articulator of conservative philosophies. In contrast, Miers had never sat on the bench, had no background in constitutional law and had never been an outspoken proponent of conservative views. Influential commentators on the right, such as Ann Coulter and George Will, denounced the choice; Coulter said the pick reflected "stunning arrogance" on the part of Bush. Many questioned Miers' loyalty to the litmus test of conservative values, the overturning of *Roe v. Wade*. Meanwhile, Senators on both sides of the aisle who met with Miers prior to her hearings declared themselves far from impressed.

On Oct. 27 the White House cut its losses: Miers with-

CHARLES DHARAPAK—AP/WIDE WORLD

ON DECK: JUDGE SAMUEL A. ALITO JR.

Born in Trenton, N.J., Alito attended Princeton University and Yale Law School and worked in the U.S. Solicitor General's office in the 1980s. A federal Appeals Court judge since 1990, Alito holds strongly conservative views that are documented in scores of opinions on everything from abortion (he wrote in favor of a Pennsylvania law that required women to notify their husbands before having an abortion) to matters of church and the state (he ruled in 1999 that a Christmas display on city property did not violate separation of church and state doctrine because it included a large plastic Santa Claus as well as religious symbols).

Alito, 55, has been dubbed "Scalito" because his opinions often resemble those of Justice Antonin Scalia. But the "another white guy" label may be his major liability in the confirmation process: in choosing Alito, President Bush gave up his onetime goal of creating a more diverse court by finding a woman or Hispanic to occupy Justice Sandra Day O'Connor's seat.

drew her name from nomination. The following Monday, Bush named a new nominee, Samuel A. Alito Jr., who has compiled an extensive record of strongly conservative rulings over the decades. His selection was quickly greeted with unanimous praise from those on the right, while those on the left vowed they would strongly oppose his ascent to the court. The battle to confirm Alito will take place after this book goes to press—and it promises to be the three-way showdown involving the White House, the Congress and the Supreme Court that partisans on both sides of America's red-state/blue-state divide have been anticipating with such intensity for so many years. ■

MATTHEW CAVANAUGH—POOL/GETTY IMAGES

THE SHORT, STRANGE TRIP OF HARRIET MIERS

On Oct. 3, President George W. Bush fulfilled his goal of naming a woman to replace Justice Sandra Day O'Connor on the Supreme Court by choosing White House counsel Harriet Miers as his nominee. Twenty-five days later, after meeting a firestorm of criticism, Miers withdrew her nomination.

Miers, a Texas native, was a math major at Southern Methodist University; she became one of nine women in a class of 143 to graduate from S.M.U. Law School in 1970. She clerked for two years for a Texas district judge, then joined a large Dallas law firm. A pioneer, she was the first woman president of her firm, of the Dallas bar, then of the Texas state bar. Raised a Catholic, Miers joined an Evangelical church in 1979. She met George W. Bush at a gala dinner in 1989 and became his legal counsel when he ran for Governor in 1994; he then named her to fix the scandal-ridden Texas Lottery Commission. Her first post at the Bush White House was staff secretary; she took over as counsel when Alberto Gonzales became Attorney General. Like 41 of the 109 Supreme Court Justices in U.S. history, she had never served as a judge.

Conservatives opposed Miers because she was not far enough on the right, but her inexperience fed the most serious charge against her confirmation: that she was a judicial lightweight, poorly versed on the constitutional issues that are the high court's chief focus. As she made the rounds of Senate offices prior to the confirmation hearings, she failed to win friends and influence people. "She needs a crash course in constitutional law," said Arlen Specter, the Republican chairman of the Senate Judiciary Committee. Some Senators professed themselves dismayed by Miers' inability to discuss key precedents and cases that are well established signposts in U.S. judicial history; others said they were startled to find that Miers gushed effusively about the President's abilities but had little to say for her own.

THE U.S. IN IRAQ

MORE TESTING, MORE SACRIFICE

ON DEC. 18, 2005, AS THE DEATH TOLL FOR U.S. TROOPS in Iraq stood at 2,158, President George W. Bush spoke to the nation in a televised address from the Oval Office. Repeating the themes he had sounded in a quartet of speeches leading up to the Dec. 15 national elections in Iraq, the President squarely faced the difficult U.S. position there, where some 159,000 U.S. troops confronted a powerful insurgency movement that seemed to be impossible to quell, even as the nation was succeeding in taking its first halting steps toward democracy. The President, reprising points he had sounded in his earlier addresses, admitted that the decision to intervene in Iraq had been based on faulty intelligence and that the work of reconstructing the nation "has been especially difficult—more difficult than we had expected." Yet he urged Americans to support the effort, declaring, "Our work is not done. There is more testing and sacrifice before us."

That was a clear-eyed assessment of the future rather than a sugar-coated dose of spin—but would Americans rally around the President's plea? As the U.S. intervention in Iraq ground on toward its third anniversary in March 2006, the mission was a bewildering amalgam of promise and pain. Even as three successful elections brought an increasing number of Iraqis into the democratic process, the daily drumbeat of insurgent attacks continued, raising more and more questions about the war's origins and conduct and increasing calls for a realistic U.S. exit strategy.

For most of the year, polls showed that support among Americans for the war was steadily declining. But the President's December speeches began to reverse the slide, and even the New York *Times* editorial page, a frequent critic of the conduct of the war, hailed the Dec. 15 elections as a "triumph." Yet in that same week, when the Bush Administration should have been celebrating a major political victory in Iraq, the President was stymied by the U.S. Senate, which refused to grant an extension of the Patriot Act, and Bush was also forced to sign on to an antitorture policy sponsored by Senator and former POW John McCain that the White House had bitterly opposed.

Iraqis Go to the Polls On the political front, several crucial milestones were achieved in 2005 in the struggle to transform Iraq's onetime dictatorship into a modern democracy.

WATHIQ KHUZAIE—GETTY IMAGES

RUINS A U.S. soldier patrols the scene of a car-bomb explosion in a Shi'ite neighborhood in Baghdad on May 23 that killed three people and injured 70

War of Nerves: Bullets and Ballots

Like all guerrilla warriors, the insurgents in Iraq sought to wear down U.S. and coalition forces, as well as political support for the war in the U.S., by a steady stream of small attacks. This timeline shows only a fraction of the 2005 strikes, as well as the year's key political advances.

Jan. 2
A suicide car bomber targets a bus carrying Iraqi troops from Baghdad, killing 26 and wounding 6.

Jan. 4
Ali Al-Haidri, Governor of Baghdad province, is assassinated along with two of his bodyguards.

Jan. 12
Two aides to Iraq's most senior Shi'ite cleric, Grand Ayatullah Ali al-Sistani, are assassinated.

Jan. 19
At least 26 are killed in Baghdad in bombings at the Australian embassy, a bank, a police station and a military complex.

Jan. 25
Judge Qais Hashim Shameri and his son are killed in an ambush in eastern Baghdad; 11 Iraqi policemen are killed in a separate incident. Five U.S. soldiers are killed when their armored vehicle rolls into a canal during a sandstorm.

Jan. 26
A U.S. Marine helicopter crash and attacks around Iraq leave a total of 37 U.S. troops dead.

Jan. 29
On election eve, about 17 people die from car bombs, and a rocket hits the U.S. embassy compound in Baghdad's fortified Green Zone, killing two Americans.

Jan. 30
Braving more than 260 attacks, some 8 million people vote to elect Iraq's Transitional National Assembly, below. Many Sunni Muslims boycott the vote, at their leaders' urging.

SASA KRALJ—AP/WIDE WORLD

Feb. 7
Two suicide bombers in Mosul and Baquba kill 27 Iraqis.

Feb. 8
At least 21 people are killed in a blast at an Iraqi army center in west Baghdad.

Feb. 10
At least 50 Iraqis are killed in attacks across the country.

Feb. 11
More than 20 Iraqis are killed in attacks near a Shi'ite mosque and at a Baghdad bakery.

Feb. 12
A car-bomb attack kills at least 17 people in the town of Musayyib.

Feb. 19
At least 40 people are killed and more than 100 wounded by suicide bombers during the Islamic festival of Ashoura.

Feb. 24
A suicide car bomber dressed as a policeman blows himself up, killing 12 Iraqis in Tikrit.

Feb. 28
At least 115 people die when a suicide bomber drives a car into a line of men waiting to join the Iraqi army and police force in Baghdad. Another 130 are wounded in a blast in Hilla, below, about 60 miles southeast of Baghdad.

March 5
U.S. soldiers shoot at a car carrying Giuliana Sgrena, an Italian journalist just released from captivity by Iraqi insurgents; she is wounded, and an Italian intelligence agent is killed. Ten days later Italy says it will withdraw all its troops from Iraq.

March 7
More than 30 people are killed and dozens are wounded in attacks in Baquba and Baghdad.

March 10
At least 47 people are killed by a suicide bomber at a Shi'ite funeral service in Mosul.

March 20
Near Baghdad, 24 rebels are

CRATER Improvised explosive devices, or IEDs , placed on roadways were among the deadliest weapons of the insurgents. This Aug. 4 blast at Barwana killed 14 Marines and a civilian interpreter

On Jan. 30, 8 million Iraqis, 58% of those eligible, braved widespread incidents of violence and went to the polls to elect 275 members of a Transitional National Assembly. Days after the vote, Iraqis were still waving index fingers stained with the dark ink that proved they had taken part. Yet millions of Iraqis chose not to vote: most Sunni Muslims boycotted the elections at their leaders' urging, on the ground that participation meant acknowledging the legitimacy of the event. As Sunnis stood passive on the sidelines, their historical dominance of Iraqi politics seemed to end in a whimper.

Two months later, the Transitional National Assembly formed a government, choosing Kurdish leader Jalal Talabani to serve as interim President and Shi'ite Ibrahim al-Jaafari as Prime Minister. In August members of the assembly and leaders of the executive branch completed negotiations over the draft of a new constitution, after deadlocking over such issues as the extent of Kurdish autonomy in the north and Shi'ite autonomy in the south and the role of Islamic law in the state.

On Oct. 15 Iraqi voters returned to the polls for a referendum in which they approved the new constitution by a 78% majority. This time around, more Sunnis went to the polls: their leaders had belatedly realized that if they were to have any say in the future of the country, they must begin to take part in the democratic process. Their participation was secured after Shi'ites and Kurds, under pressure from the U.S., agreed to amend the constitution upon its successful adoption to make it more inclusive.

"Our work is not done. There is more testing and sacrifice before us." —George W. Bush

The January and October votes cleared the way for a more significant milestone: the national elections on Dec. 15, in which Iraqi voters chose a permanent government. On that historic day, the polls in Iraq stayed open an hour after the scheduled closing time to accommodate a surge in voter turnout all over the country. A more diverse group of Iraqis walked out of polling stations with the iconic ink-stained finger than in the year's earlier elections—a clear sign that the parliament emerging from the vote will reflect a wider spectrum of the nation's people.

The big news was the heavy participation of Sunni voters, whose political leaders again urged them to turn out in large numbers. Some insurgent websites even called for a moratorium on attacks at polling stations so Sunni voters wouldn't be scared away. Indeed, the biggest surprise of the day was the absence of insurgent attacks. As polls closed across Iraq, Arabic news channels had yet to report a single attack on a polling station

ALI ABU SHISH—REUTERS

JACOB SILBERBERG—AP/WIDE WORLD

anywhere in the country. Islam Online, a popular website that posts news about the insurgency, reported that insurgents in restive Anbar province were even seen manning checkpoints to protect voters from attacks by al-Qaeda elements. In Saddam Hussein's hometown of Tikrit, locals described long lines and no major attacks. The polling centers in Fallujah were overwhelmed by the participation, locals told TIME.

Saddam on Trial The U.S. had another cause for optimism in 2005: the trial of Saddam Hussein finally began. On Oct. 19 the former strongman, 68, appeared in a Baghdad courtroom before a panel of five judges. Saddam and seven associates faced charges in the torture and killing of 148 men and boys after an assassination attempt against him in 1982 in Dujail, a Shi'ite town near Baghdad.

Saddam refused to confirm his name, expressed his defiance of "this so-called court" and finally pleaded not guilty. At one point in December, the former dictator simply failed to appear for the proceedings, but the case continued, with his chair empty.

The Insurgents Even as the political and judicial fronts offered promise, insurgent forces continued their war of nerves on Iraqis. The insurgents—a many-headed aggregation of Sunni Iraqis and foreign jihadists that included al-Qaeda agents—attacked not only U.S. and coalition troops but also the nation's infrastructure, aiming to make life difficult for all while U.S. troops were still in the land. By early summer, a report from the Iraqi Interior Ministry concluded that civilians and police officers were being killed at a rate of more than 800 a month—or about one every hour, 24 hours a day.

In June General John Abizaid, the top U.S. commander in Iraq, testified before Congress that the strength of the insurgency had not diminished during the first half of 2005 and that it was poised to grow stronger. "I believe there are more foreign fighters coming into Iraq than there were six months ago," Abizaid said. His opinion contradicted the view of Vice President Dick Cheney, who made headlines days earlier when he said that "the level of activity that we see today from a military standpoint ... will clearly decline. I think they're in the last throes, if you will, of the insurgency."

One dissenter from that view was a high-ranking U.S. officer who told TIME's Michael Ware, "We have not broken the back of the insurgency. [It's] like a cell-phone system. You shut down one node, another somewhere else comes online to replace it."

The year's largest U.S. assault on insurgent forces took place in September in Tall 'Afar. Close to Syria, the town is at the center of a vast border region that is a gateway for foreign fighters entering Iraq. The attack sent some 7,000 U.S. and Iraqi soldiers and hundreds of Bradley fighting vehicles, tanks and artillery pieces—combined with AC-130 Spectre gunships, F-16 fighter jets and attack helicopters—to roust insurgents from the area. But as with most direct assaults against the insurgents, it was difficult to say whether the coalition forces had won a major victory or had merely scattered their foes momentarily.

KARIM KADIM—AP/WIDE WOR_D

KARIM KADIM—AP/WIDE WORLD

killed in a gun battle. Earlier, a suicide bomber kills the top police officer in the anticorruption department in Mosul. Attacks at his funeral kill at least two people.

March 24
Iraqi special police commandos, backed by U.S. troops and helicopters, raid what they say is a "major terror training camp" in the heart of the Sunni triangle.

March 26
Insurgents strike back, killing 11 Iraqi police commandos and four female translators working for the U.S. military.

April 6
The new Iraq Assembly selects Kurdish leader Jalal Talabani, below, as President. The next day, Shi'ite Ibrahim al-Jaafari is named Prime Minister.

April 4
Insurgents attack Baghdad's Abu Ghraib prison, wounding at least 44 U.S. troops and 12 prisoners.

April 9
Two years after Saddam's fall, tens of thousands of Iraqis loyal to Shi'ite cleric Muqtada al-Sadr march through Baghdad denouncing the U.S. occupation.

April 14
Two car bombs kill 18 in Baghdad.

April 18
Gunmen ambush a senior Defense Ministry adviser, Major General Adnan al-Qaraghulli, killing him and his son.

April 19
Two U.S. soldiers are killed and four wounded in a car bombing. Other attacks kill a dozen people and wound more than 50.

April 20
Former interim Prime Minister Iyad Allawi escapes an assassination attempt that kills two policeman and wounds four.

April 21
A U.S. commercial helicopter is shot down north of Baghdad, killing 11 U.S. civilian contractors.

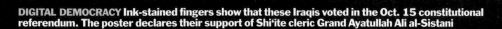

DIGITAL DEMOCRACY Ink-stained fingers show that these Iraqis voted in the Oct. 15 constitutional referendum. The poster declares their support of Shi'ite cleric Grand Ayatullah Ali al-Sistani

April 23
Nine Iraqi and four U.S. soldiers are killed when troop convoys are attacked near Baghdad.

May 1
A suicide attack in Tal 'Afar kills at least 25 people and injures 30.

May 2
Twelve die in Baghdad bombings.

May 4
At least 60 people are killed and dozens wounded in a suicide bombing in Erbil, northern Iraq.

May 5
At least 24 people die in a wave of attacks in Baghdad.

May 6
A suicide car bomber strikes a market in Suwayra, a Shi'ite Muslim town south of Baghdad, killing 58 and wounding 44.

May 7
Two suicide car bombs explode in central Baghdad, killing 22.

May 11
At least 71 people are killed and more than 160 wounded when at least five explosions rock Tikrit, Hawija and Baghdad.

May 12
Police General Iyad Imad Mehdi is killed in Baghdad driving to work.

May 23
In a series of attacks across the country, including in Baghdad, below, 49 Iraqis die.

June 17
In Operation Spear, 1,000 U.S. Marines, backed by warplanes, launch a major hunt for insurgents on Iraq's border with Syria.

July 7
Al-Qaeda executes kidnapped Egyptian envoy Ihab al-Sherif, 51.

June 17
A suicide bomb blows up a fuel truck near Baghdad, killing 100.

July 24
A suicide truck bomber strikes in Baghdad, killing 40.

Aug. 3
A roadside bomb kills 14 Marines close to the Syrian border.

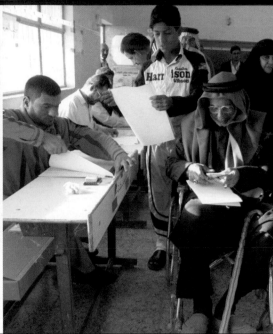

PROTEST AND PROGRESS The November call by Representative John Murtha, left, for a rapid withdrawal of U.S. troops rocked the White House, but Bush pointed to the Dec. 15 Iraqi elections as a hopeful sign

The Home Front For Americans watching from far away, the daily news of improvised explosive devices and suicide bombings marched in lockstep with frequent reminders of the war's questionable rationale and ongoing concerns that it was being conducted ethically. In March, a commission appointed by Bush in 2004 to investigate the intelligence that led to the decision to invade concluded that U.S. spy agencies were "dead wrong" in their assessments that Iraq harbored weapons of mass destruction and called the lapse "a major intelligence failure."

On May 1, the London *Sunday Times* published the "Downing Street Memo," leaked minutes from a July 23, 2002, meeting that included British Prime Minister Tony Blair in which it was noted, eight months before the 2003 invasion, that "Bush had already made up his mind to take military action, even if the timing was not yet decided." The memo quoted the chief of the Secret Intelligence Service as saying, "The intelligence and facts were being fixed around the policy."

By Oct. 25, a Harris poll indicated for the first time that a majority of Americans had come to believe that invading and occupying Iraq were the "wrong thing to do."

On Nov. 17, the White House was blindsided by a surprising new voice: Democratic Congressman John Murtha of Pennsylvania, who had been a consistent hawk on Iraq. Murtha, a twice-wounded and much decorated Marine Vietnam veteran, called a press conference in which he recounted meeting

with wounded Iraq veterans. Choking up as he described a soldier who lost both his hands, Murtha concluded, "Our military's done everything that has been asked of them. The U.S. cannot accomplish anything further in Iraq militarily. It's time to bring the troops home."

Republicans in Congress were quick to slam Murtha with words like coward and traitor, but his background and evident sincerity struck a chord with the public. Dialing back the partisan attack, Vice President Cheney quickly called Murtha "a good man, a Marine, a patriot," who was "taking a clear stand in an entirely legitimate discussion." But the Administration continued its full-court press against other Democrats voicing doubts about the war.

Questions of Torture The year also brought reminders of the moral cost of the war in the form of a slew of guilty verdicts in the trials of former guards at Abu Ghraib prison and new charges of prisoner abuse at detention centers in Iraq. By fall the Administration was under fire on the issue of torture, which critics charged had become standard U.S. policy in the war on terrorism. Senator John McCain, who was himself tortured while a POW in Vietnam, introduced legislation banning cruel, inhumane or degrading treatment of prisoners in U.S. custody, which put Administration officials in the awkward position of arguing for an exemption for CIA agents. The measure was approved by the Senate in October by a 90-to-9 vote.

The controversy over human-rights issues

escalated in early November when the Washington *Post* revealed that the CIA had been operating a secret prison system for almost four years that included eight covert detention facilities in Eastern Europe and Asia. Those "black sites" were used to house al-Qaeda members secretly abducted from countries around the world since Sept. 11, 2001. European officials expressed dismay that prisoners might have been abducted within or transported through their territory in secret; several countries opened investigations into whether U.S. agents had broken their laws. The charges gained new momentum when two secret prisons run by the Iraqi

"I think they're in the last throes, so to speak, of the insurgency." —Vice President Dick Cheney

Interior Ministry were raided by U.S. forces, who found that detainees had been beaten, starved, burned and abused in other ways.

The issue clouded a pair of trips to Europe by Secretary of State Condoleezza Rice in November and December, which became pilgrimages of explanation. On Dec. 15, the same day that Iraqis voted for their new government, President Bush joined Senator McCain at the White House to declare he would embrace McCain's antitorture measure. It was a clear defeat for the Administration.

The next day Bush was again rebuffed by the Senate, which refused to extend the Patriot Act, a centerpiece of the Administration's war on terrorism on the home front, after the New York *Times* reported that since 2001 he had authorized secret wiretaps on U.S. citizens by the National Security Agency

without first obtaining legal court warrants.

In December the reeling White House attacked the growing crisis in confidence head-on. In his series of speeches, Bush outlined a strategy for success. He claimed there were signs of real progress: more Iraqi and police combat battalions deployed in the field and more Iraqi participation in combat, even when led by Americans. Such advances, he said, would lead to the beginning of a drawback by U.S. troops into large, remote bases outside the major cities, where they would be less vulnerable to attack by insurgents. By mid-December Bush's approval rating registered at 40%, up from a low of 35% a month earlier.

AKRAM SALEH—GETTY IMAGES

The Horizon The year's events showed steady progress toward a democratic Iraq, but also clarified the reality of the beleaguered U.S. soldiers there: they faced an unending fight against a seemingly inexhaustible enemy emboldened by the U.S. presence, the measure of success as elusive as the foes themselves.

The Bush Administration confronts hard questions in Iraq. Can political success be salvaged from a military fight that may be unwinnable? Can the U.S. extract itself without harming its interests in the region? Can Iraqis ever guarantee their own security? Can Shi'ites, Kurds and Sunnis, trained in the school of enmity, ever embrace a common destiny? As 2006 approached, the answers carried a price tag—more testing and more sacrifice—that the U.S. public seemed increasingly hesitant to pay. ∎

A RISING TIDE OF DISSENT

Cindy Sheehan, 48, began a one-woman vigil on the road leading to President Bush's Crawford, Texas, ranch during his August vacation, asking that the President meet with her and explain what was being gained in Iraq that justified the cost of her son's life. Casey Sheehan, 24, was killed along with six other soldiers in Sadr City on April 4, 2004, less than a month after he arrived in Iraq. Sheehan's stakeout caught the nation's attention, and an informal camp of antiwar activists, including several other mothers of fallen soldiers, soon sprang up in the area. Bush resolutely refused to see her; the two had already met before Sheehan's antiwar stance hardened. As more Americans grew doubtful about the lagging progress of the Iraq mission, a September march in Washington attracted a crowd of some 150,000 antiwar protesters.

TAYLOR JOSEPH—GETTY IMAGES

Aug. 31
Some 1,000 people die in a stampede on Baghdad's Al-Aaimmah bridge, below, after rumors of a suicide bomber cause panic among religious pilgrims.

Sept. 14
More than 150 people are killed as attacks target Shi'ite Muslims in Baghdad. Al-Qaeda claims responsibility for the violence.

Sept. 19
British military units clash directly with Iraqi police in Basra in a flare-up involving two captured British soldiers.

Oct. 15
Some 9 million Iraqis vote in the constitutional referendum, approving the document.

Oct. 24
Sixteen people die in a major strike on Baghdad's Palestine Hotel, where many foreign journalists quarter.

Nov. 5
U.S. and Iraqi troops mount a major offensive against the town of Husayba, near the Syrian border.

Nov. 10
A suicide bomber kills 30 in a Baghdad café.

Nov. 18
Suicide bombers kill 70 in northeastern Iraq. The next day, a car bombing at a funeral kills 30 more people. More attacks over the weekend bring the three-day toll to more than 150.

Nov. 24
A suicide bomber kills more than 30 people in Mahmudiya.

Dec. 3
Ten U.S. Marines are killed by an IED on the outskirts of Fallujah.

Dec. 6
Two suicide bombs kill 36 at Baghdad's police academy.

Dec. 8
A suicide bomber kills more than 30 in Baghdad's bus terminal.

NationNotebook

Fourscore and Seven Beards Ago

Honest Abe impersonators gather to celebrate the opening of the Abraham Lincoln Presidential Museum in Springfield, Ill. The $115 million complex, which opened in April as the only presidential library run by a state government, holds 1,500 manuscripts, including a copy of the Gettysburg Address in Lincoln's hand. The glitzy museum features a special-effects parade of ghostly holograms and Lincoln mannequins, leading some scholars to charge it is dedicated more to razzle-dazzle than education. One charged: it's "Six Flags over Lincoln."

❝ I am married to the President of the United States, and here is our typical evening: 9 o'clock, Mr. Excitement here is fast asleep. Ladies and gentlemen, I am a desperate housewife. **❞**

—**LAURA BUSH**, *First Lady, at a press corps dinner*

The Washington Waltz

Three men who have held major positions in the capital left their old jobs in 2005 to take on new assignments. Two of them, Bolton and Wolfowitz, are controversial figures who are highly regarded by President Bush.

John Bolton
George W. Bush wanted Bolton, a conservative diplomat who has long scorned the United Nations, to be the U.S. ambassador to the U.N. When the Senate balked, Bush appointed Bolton while Congress was out of session.

Paul Wolfowitz
One of the principal architects of the U.S. intervention in Iraq, controversy magnet Wolfowitz traded in guns for butter, leaving his Pentagon post as Deputy Secretary of Defense to become head of the World Bank.

Ben S. Bernanke
The Princeton University economics professor, a former member of the Federal Reserve Board, was appointed by the President in October to the unenviable task of filling the shoes of legendary Fed chief Alan Greenspan.

Deep Thoughts

Who was that masked man? In their best-selling 1974 book *All the President's Men*, reporters Bob Woodward and Carl Bernstein cloaked the identity of the source who gave them their best leads in the Watergate scandal as Deep Throat. Hal Holbrook played the role of the informant in the 1976 movie. On May 31, after 33 years of mystery, W. Mark Felt, a former FBI official who is now 91, declared that he was Deep Throat in a *Vanity Fair* article. Felt suffered a stroke in 2001; family members said they wanted the world to know of his role before he died.

CLOCKWISE FROM TOP: RICHARD DREW—AP/WIDE WORLD; RON EDMONDS—AP/WIDE WORLD; CHARLES DHARAPAK—AP/WIDE WORLD; BEN MARGOT—AP/WIDE WORLD

Police Blotter

The top crime stories of 2005 seemed sadly, achingly familiar: a serial killer and sexual pervert finally confessed to a heinous string of murders, while a troubled teen who had posted his mental problems on the Internet shot up his high school.

DENNIS RADER Rader, 60, who called himself BTK, for "bind, torture, kill," confessed to murdering 10 people in Wichita, Kans., between 1974 and 1991. He was given ten consecutive life terms in prison.

JEFF WEISE On March 21, Weise, 16, shot and killed nine people, seven of them at his high school, on the Red Lake Indian reservation in Minnesota, then took his own life. He was age 9 in the picture at right.

BART ROSS Ross, 57, angry at Chicago federal judge Joan Lefkow for dismissing a malpractice suit, killed her husband and mother on Feb. 28, then shot himself in March.

FROM TOP: JEFF TUTTLE—AP/WIDE WORLD; KARE-TV—AP/WIDE WORLD; NAM Y. HUH—AP/WIDE WORLD

MATT ARCHER—GETTY IMAGES

Drawing Board

THEY'RE SHOOTING LOOTERS... RUN FOR IT.

$231 MILLION ALASKAN BRIDGE TO NOWHERE

HWY BILL $

© 05 AKRON BEACON JOURNAL

CHIP BOK-AKRON BEACON JOURNAL-CREATORS SYNDICATE

Arnold Under Fire

Hollywood hero Arnold Schwarzenegger rode a wave of voter discontent to become Governor of California in late 2003, but he stumbled badly in 2005. In November California voters resoundingly rejected four ballot initiatives he had strongly pushed, involving teachers' tenure, public-sector unions, the redistricting of congressional seats and state budget caps. The rejections were a stinging rebuke for the Governor, whose approval ratings have fallen from 61% in 2004 to 33% in 2005.

KEVORK DJANSEZIAN—AP/WIDE WORLD

In U.S. Army Courtrooms, Echoes of Abu Ghraib

In a series of trials and investigations, the U.S. military struggled to assign accountability for the abuses in the Abu Ghraib prison in Baghdad, first seen in a series of pictures that shocked the world when published in April 2004. The ringleader of the abusers, Army reservist Charles Graner, was found guilty on Jan. 14 of charges including conspiracy to maltreat detainees and committing indecent acts; he was sentenced to 10 years in prison. Graner is the father of an out-of-wedlock child with Private Lynndie England, left, seen restraining a naked Iraqi with a leash in one notorious picture. After a mistrial in May, England was convicted, given a dishonorable discharge and sentenced to three years in jail in September. In charges against those higher up the chain of command, the Army cleared four top officers of wrongdoing in April. The most senior officer to be reprimanded was Brigadier General Janis Karpinski, the commanding officer of Graner and England, who was demoted in May.

A FRENZY OF PROTEST ROCKS FRANCE

The accidental deaths in late October of a pair of teenagers who thought they were being pursued by police touched off weeks of violent protests in the mean streets of the banlieues, or suburbs, that ring France's major cities. The rioters were mostly Arab or black, but they were also mostly French, the children and grandchildren of immigrants from former colonies, born and bred in the neighborhoods they were setting ablaze. The rage expressed by the alienated young people dealt a crushing blow to France's self-image as a model of tolerance and social equality, even as it revealed a government that seemed incapable of keeping order. Above all, it exposed the nation's desperate shortage of *égalité* and *fraternité*: unemployment in some of the suburbs runs higher than 40%.

REMY DE LA MAUVINIERE—AP/ WIDE WORLD

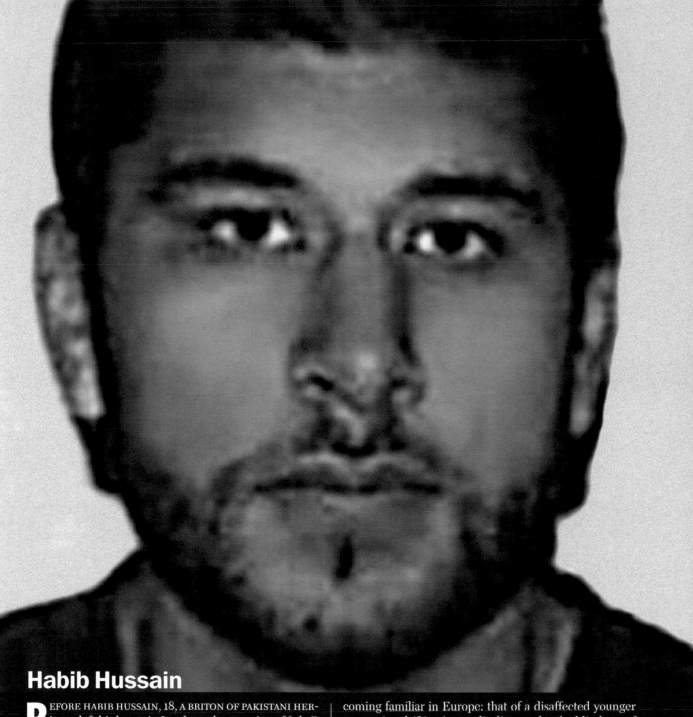

Habib Hussain

BEFORE HABIB HUSSAIN, 18, A BRITON OF PAKISTANI HER-itage, left his home in Leeds on the morning of July 7, he told his parents he was going to spend the day in London with friends. At 8:50 a.m., bombs rocked three trains on London's Underground; 57 minutes later, a bus was blown apart. Fifty-six people were dead, more than 700 injured. Some 12 hours later, Hussain's mother called a police hot line and reported her son missing; she feared he might have been injured in the bombings. She was right. Her son had blown up the bus—and himself.

How did it come to this? It is often tempting to conclude that those who purposely commit suicide in the service of mass slaughter must be sick, evil, not quite human; they are not us. But now Britons were forced to confront the fact that the killers were their own: they were soccer-playing, cricket-loving young men who seemed, on the surface, utterly normal. A deeper look tells a darker story that is be-coming familiar in Europe: that of a disaffected younger generation drifting into radicalism under the blind eye of immigrant parents, slowly giving up its energies to groups whose zeal and camaraderie offer a sense of purpose. There its members are talent-spotted by jihadists for deep-er indoctrination—and finally groomed for murder.

Tall and a bit of a clown, Hussain was a mediocre student. After he got into some fights at his racially divided school, he went to Mecca on a pilgrimage with his father, who then sent him to study in Pakistan, hoping the teen would gain discipline. When Hussain returned to Leeds, he grew a beard and began dressing in traditional Muslim clothes. Within a year, he was dead by his own hand.

How did it come to this? Like the snapshot above, our image of Hussain remains blurry. Yet we cannot hope to defuse the death-dreams of Islam's suicidal young terrorists until we bring our vision of them into sharper focus. ∎

Tony Blair

I GET KNOCKED DOWN, BUT I get up again," the British pop band Chumbawamba sang back in 1997, the year Tony Blair electrified Britain by leading his Labour Party to its first election victory since 1974. Eight years later, Blair is still marching to Chumbawamba's beat: his 2005 was a vertiginous rush of highs and lows that required all his intellect and energy to navigate. Blair's support for George W. Bush's Iraq policy has cost him dearly with British voters; polls show that many regard him as a liar. So when he won a third term in May, it should have been a moment of triumph; instead, he limped across the finish line with his majority in Parliament sharply reduced, from 166 seats to 65.

Blair had big plans for July: as host of the annual G-8 summit, he planned to address one his major priorities, debt relief for Africa. On July 5, the day before the summit convened in Scotland, Blair made a quick trip to Singapore, where the International Olympic Committee was meeting to choose the site of the 2012 Games. Blair lobbied for London—and the next day, he learned that the British capital had won the nod. The elated PM joined Britons in impromptu celebrations, then went to Scotland—only to be called back to London the next morning to deal with the horrific July 7 terrorist bombings that killed 56 people. In the first hours of crisis Blair stood tall, declaring, "When they try to intimidate us, we will not be intimidated. When they seek to change our country or our way of life by these methods, we will not be changed." It was one of his finest hours. But in November the PM got knocked down again: scores of Labour backbenchers deserted him on a vote to stiffen Britain's antiterrorism laws, and the measure failed—a clear sign that his days in power may be nearing an end. Unless he gets up again. ∎

ADRIAN DENNIS—GETTY IMAGES

Mahmoud Abbas

HIS HONEYMOON DIDN'T LAST LONG. ON Jan. 9, Mahmoud Abbas was elected Palestinian President, taking over the post held by the late Yasser Arafat, and he received a congratulatory phone call from Israel's Prime Minister, Ariel Sharon. Four days later, Palestinian militants killed six Israelis at a freight crossing point between Israel and the Gaza Strip. Sharon, who knows and trusts Abbas, suspended ties with the Palestinian Authority the next day. The message: Abbas must act fast to rein in Palestine's militant groups, Hamas, Islamic Jihad and the Aqsa Martyrs Brigades of Abbas' own P.L.O. Fatah Party.

Abbas quickly sent his police into parts of the Gaza Strip that had been in the hands of the militants for years. The show of force impressed Sharon: early in February, he and Abbas signed the agreement that led to Israel's historic summer withdrawal from 21 settlements in the Gaza Strip and 4 in the West Bank. Yet the militant factions, rather than his Fatah party, appear to be increasingly popular among Palestinians: in December elections in West Bank towns, Hamas candidates far outpolled Fatah candidates.

Abbas, 69, has worked long and hard for this moment. Born in Safed, a town now part of Israel, he grew up in Damascus after his family fled when the Jewish state was founded in 1948. As a young member of Fatah, he made his name as a fund raiser, avoiding involvement in terrorist attacks. He was among the first Fatah leaders to build bridges to Israeli peace campaigners; in 1977 he issued a declaration in favor of a two-state solution, a break from P.L.O. doctrine, which called for the eradication of Israel. Abbas' ties with Israeli officials made him a key architect of the secret negotiations that produced the Oslo peace accord in 1993. Twelve years later, he is still the quintessential man in the middle, a moderate working for peace in a region where violence has long seemed the only answer to every question. ■

EASTNEWS—GAMMA PRESS

Viktor Yushchenko

FOR UKRAINE'S NEW PRESIDENT, 2005 WAS THE MONDAY after the Miracle. In 2004 Viktor Yushchenko survived both a slow-motion assassination attempt in the form of dioxin poisoning and a rigged election that drove his supporters into the streets to demand a new vote. The result was the Orange Revolution that released Russia's grip on the nation. After rising to power on this giddy wave of democratic exuberance, the populist hero found himself facing a passel of more quotidian concerns: official corruption at home, the new fault lines with Russia, the need to make a reborn Ukraine attractive to Western investors.

Some of Yushchenko's attempts at reform were powerfully symbolic. In July he fired all Ukraine's 23,000 traffic police, notorious for fabricating reasons to stop motorists in order to demand bribes. But more challenging reforms, like the privatization of government-owned industries and the passage of legislation guaranteeing property rights, slowed to a near halt, in part due to an ongoing rivalry between the centrist Yushchenko and his left-leaning prime minister, Yulia Tymoshenko. The stalemate also scared off much needed foreign investment into the country.

Looming above all was the age-old question of Russia: Yushchenko's distinct Westward tilt is seen by President Vladimir Putin as a serious threat. Two weeks after his stunning December 2004 election, Yushchenko was told that neighboring Turkmenistan was shutting off a pipeline that delivers more than 75% of Ukraine's natural gas. The crisis (probably triggered at Putin's behest) was soon resolved—but not until Ukraine agreed to pay an additional $500 million for its gas.

On Sept. 8, Yushchenko took decisive action: he fired his entire government, setting up a potential showdown between himself and Tymoshenko in elections slated for March 2006. Will his gambit work? "If this country is governed by honest people and the government can survive, people will feel the effects of the economic development plan within a year," Yushchenko told his people after taking office. As he learned in 2005, that's a very large if. ∎

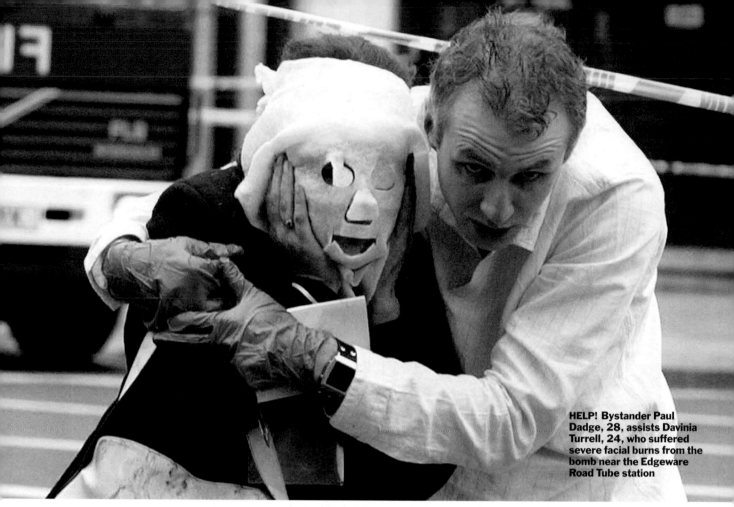

JANE MINGAY—AP/WIDE WORLD

HELP! Bystander Paul Dadge, 28, assists Davinia Turrell, 24, who suffered severe facial burns from the bomb near the Edgeware Road Tube station

A NEW BATTLE OF BRITAIN

A quartet of suicide bombers strikes, and the United Kingdom joins the nations targeted by Islamists who wield terror as their weapon

ON JULY 6, 2005, LONDON WAS AT THE TOP OF ITS GAME. Fresh from playing host to the Wimbledon tennis tournament and a Live 8 concert in Hyde Park that drew an audience of more than 200,000, residents of Britain's capital got the good news that their city had won the right to hold the Olympic Games in 2012, beating out rivals that included Paris and New York City. With the city's population growing, its economy booming and its modern image as a tolerantly multicultural global hot spot newly reinforced, Londoners were feeling chipper.

So the worse-than-usual traffic on the Thursday morning of July 7 didn't trouble George Psaradakis, 49, as he drove the No. 30 double-decker red bus through the streets of Bloomsbury. Congested streets, after all, are just another sign of a thriving city's healthy thrum. But as he approached Tavistock Square, Psaradakis could see that something was wrong. Thousands of commuters had left Underground train stations and were milling about the streets looking for alternative ways to get to work. Some of them were talking about a fire in the tunnel below, but nobody seemed to have clear idea of what had happened.

What had happened, moments earlier, was that London had joined the ranks of New York City, Bali, Jakarta,

Karachi, Riyadh, Casablanca and Madrid—targets where blood had been spilled by Islamic terrorists. And 7/7 had been added to the roster of dates (9/11 for Manhattan, 3/11 for Madrid) that are modern shorthand for horror.

Three separate bombs had been detonated on trains in London's Underground. Two of the bombs—at Aldgate and Edgware Road—were in trains just below the surface, on so-called cut-and-cover lines, so the force of the blast was dissipated into a relatively wide tunnel. Seven people died at Edgware Road and seven at Aldgate. But the bomb on the Piccadilly Line near King's Cross was in one of the Underground's deep tubes, some 100 ft. below the surface. There, the blast, with nowhere to go, had killed dozens of people, and emergency workers would later describe the scene as particularly hellish.

It wasn't over yet. As chaos spilled from the rail system into the streets, Psaradakis' bus was diverted from its usual route. At 9:47, about an hour after the three subway blasts had been detonated in the space of a minute, he stopped his bus in Tavistock Square to get directions. Just then, Lou Stein, an American theater producer who has lived in London for 20 years, heard a tremendous thud from his apartment 100 yds. away and ran outside. "It was oddly silent," he said later, with "a lot of distressed people crying into each other's arms. The top of the bus was lifted off, like the top of a tin can that's just been ripped open. There was smoke everywhere." When a TIME reporter arrived on the scene about 25 minutes later, he could see smears of blood all over the façade of the British Medical Association headquarters in the square and survivors comforting each other. Psaradakis survived, but more than a dozen others died in the explosion on his bus. Horrified witnesses told of seeing severed limbs and a body with its head blown off.

In all, 56 people were killed by the four London bombs, with more than 700 others injured, making this the worst attack on London since World War II. Within hours, police got the tip that would lead them to the bombers (*see* p. 46 and sidebar below). Britons were aghast at who had pulled off the attack, and how. These were not foreign-born militants: three of the four bombers were British natives, born to Pakistani immigrants. In a subway surveillance video, the four are seen chatting calmly 30 minutes before the first explosions, after which they fan out in different directions, prepared to meet their deaths.

The bombers were what law-enforcement officials call "cleanskins"—people with little on their records to raise suspicion. Their weapon was a homemade explosive called TATP, a material popular with al-Qaeda because it can be prepared in a bathtub out of common chemicals. The bombs weighed only 6 lbs. each, but were powerful enough to vaporize the bodies closest to the explosions, shred metal and kill people standing as far away as 100 ft.

A pall settled over London in the days that followed, but even this sullen peace was shattered two weeks later when a second wave of bomb attacks was attempted on July 21. Once again, four separate bombers fanned out through London's transit system during morning rush hour, but their plans did not include suicide, and their devices fizzled. Realizing that live suspects could still be caught, Britain's police and security agencies launched a search that was, initially, tragically ineffectual: the very next day, jumpy police shot and killed an innocent, dark-skinned Brazilian electrician on an Underground train after they had mistakenly identified him as a terrorist.

Yet within eight days the biggest manhunt in the history of British policing succeeded in nabbing the four known members of the gang believed to have attempted the July 21 bombings. Londoners breathed more easily,

PHILLIPPA PARRY—WPN

MANGLED: The No. 30 bus, its top peeled off by a bomb, sits shattered in Tavistock Square in the Bloomsbury district

until, within days, a videotape surfaced in which al-Qaeda's second in command, Ayman al-Zawahiri, boasted, "You spilled blood like rivers in our countries and we exploded volcanoes in yours ... [Prime Minister Tony] Blair's policies brought you destruction in central London and will bring you more destruction, God willing."

As Britons dig in for what may be a long war, the government is moving ahead on two fronts: working in secret to identify the entire network of conspirators believed to have assisted in both waves of bombings and lobbying for a series of new laws, reminiscent of the U.S.'s Patriot Act, that critics say will curtail basic freedoms but proponents laud as essential to making Britain more resistant to jihad. Hopefully, Londoners will not have to wait until the 2012 Summer Games to learn to celebrate again. ■

METROPOLITAN POLICE VIA AP/WIDE WORLD

THE TERRORISTS: MADE IN THE U.K.

What frightened Britons most about the four men who bombed London (captured by a surveillance camera at left) was that they were homegrown terrorists, not outside agitators. Mohammed Sidique Khan was a 30-year-old grade-school teacher with a baby daughter and a reputation for devotion to his learning-disabled students; Shahzad Tanweer, 22, was a cricket fan who worked in his family's fish-and-chips shop in Leeds; Hasib Hussain, 18, was dressed that morning like the universal teenager, in denims and a sloppy jacket. The fourth bomber, Germaine Lindsay, 19, was a Jamaican who had become a British citizen, married a British woman and had a young son; he was a man who seemed just "an ordinary Joe Bloggs to me," in the words of a neighbor

PULLING OFF A PULLOUT

In the first year of the post-Arafat era, Ariel Sharon and Mahmoud Abbas work together to return the Gaza Strip to Palestinian hands

ZIV KOREN—POLARIS. INSET: LEFTERIS PITARAKIS-AP/WIDE WORLD

IN A REGION WHERE PROGRESS IS defined as the absence of backward motion, and any forward motion is hailed as a miracle, 2005 was a year that saw much progress and several miracles. The movement was made possible by a man who wasn't there anymore: Yasser Arafat. His death in November 2004, cleared the way for two men to take bold steps toward a new era of cooperation. One was Arafat's successor, Mahmoud Abbas (see p. 64), the new president of the Palestinian Authority (PA); the other was Israel's Prime Minister Ariel Sharon, the old, once uncompromising hawk.

IN THE ARENA: Sharon and Abbas discuss Gaza at Sharm el-Sheikh in Egypt in February

Both leaders gambled their fate on Israel's 2004 pledge to begin withdrawing, in July 2005, from settlements it had occupied in the Gaza Strip since the Six-Day War in 1967. Each fought off dissenters in his own ranks. Sharon's coalition in Israel's Knesset disintegrated in early January,

and he had to patch together a new one. Meanwhile, Abbas struggled to tame armed factions, such as Hamas and Islamic Jihad, that owed him no allegiance and were opposed to any truce with Israel.

Yet the two statesmen forged ahead, meeting at a summit conference in Egypt's Sharm el-Sheikh resort on Feb. 8, where Israel reaffirmed its commitment to the Gaza pullout, promised to release several hundred Palestinian prisoners and also agreed to resume a limited handover of towns in the occupied West Bank. Weeks later, Abbas convened a Palestinian summit at which Hamas and Islamic Jihad agreed to work within the framework of the Abbas plan and promised to replace the *intifadeh* (uprising) with a *tahediyeh* (truce). Israel later agreed to suspend its program of targeted killings of Hamas leaders. As optimism swelled, President George W. Bush welcomed Abbas to

THEY'RE OUT: On Aug. 18, in one of the most dramatic shows of resistance to their forced exit, Israeli settlers barricaded on the roof of a synagogue in Kfar Darim in the Gush Katif area battle troops training water cannons on them

ROBERTO SCHMIDT—AFP—GETTY IMAGES

MOVING DAY: Trucks gather to remove Israeli possessions from Neve Dekalim. Some 8,000 Israelis moved out of Gaza

the White House in May and pledged an additional $50 million in direct aid to the Palestinians, a first for the U.S.

Then, on July 12, an Islamic Jihad suicide bomber killed five Israeli civilians in a shopping mall in Netanya, near Tel Aviv. Within days, Israel suspended the handover of towns in the West Bank and resumed its policy of targeted killings. What Israel did not do, however, was postpone the Gaza withdrawal, signaling it was willing to continue the peace process. Instead, Sharon accelerated the timetable for the pullout, in part to preclude any violence planned by Israeli settlers. On Aug. 15, the army began a forced evacuation of Jewish settlements within Gaza and resumed the transfer of control in four West Bank villages. By Sept. 1, all 21 Jewish settlements had been completely emptied without major incident, the last Israeli soldiers had left Gaza, and 38 years of occupation had come to an end.

If the moment was inspiring, the days that followed were disappointing. Hamas leaders paraded large formations of heavily armed fighters through the settlements, declaring that their armed struggle (rather than Abbas' ne-

gotiations) had wrested Gaza from Israel, trashed synagogues and pronounced themselves in charge of the area. Militant groups resumed firing rockets into Israel, and chaos broke out on the Egyptian border. Abbas once again convinced Hamas to undertake a temporary cease-fire, although the group may been persuaded as much by Israel's resumption of air strikes and attempted assassinations of its leaders as by the pleas of Abbas. None of this augured well for the PA's ability to rein in the Palestinian terrorist organizations, much less govern a sovereign state.

In Israel, the political scene was shifting rapidly. After fighting off several challenges to his leadership, Sharon decided in November to bolt from the right-wing Likud Party he helped found in 1973 and form a new centrist bloc called Kadima, Hebrew for "forward." Days earlier, Shimon Peres had been ousted from the leadership of his own Labor Party by union firebrand Amir Peretz. When the new Labor leader announced that he was pulling out of Likud's coalition government and called for new elections in March, Peres announced that he was leaving his old party and joining Sharon's new one.

As leaders on both sides of the Israeli-Palestinian divide focused on internal politics, the momentum generated by the Gaza pullout seemed to evaporate. Ongoing negotiations ground to a three-month halt over technical issues related to Gaza's border crossings. That impasse was broken only when U.S. Secretary of State Condoleezza Rice, visiting Israel to observe the 10th anniversary of the assassination of Yitzhak Rabin, oversaw round-the-clock negotiations that resulted in a compromise that will allow Palestinians relatively free access to Gaza from Egypt but will also provide security guarantees to the Israelis.

The beginning of December brought a grim reminder that the more things change in this tortured region, the more they stay the same. On Dec. 5, as Sharon and Peres prepared for the March elections and talked of devoting the last chapter of their political careers to achieving a final peace and permanent borders with the Palestinians, a suicide bomber walked into the same Netanya shopping mall where five people had been killed in July and set off an explosive device, instantly killing five more. ∎

WorldNotebook

After the Quake, a Slow-Motion Disaster

As winter approached in northern Pakistan and India, disaster experts warned that the lingering after-effects of the massive earthquake that rocked Kashmir on Oct. 8 might claim more lives than its initial shock waves. Aid efforts were hampered by the sheer remoteness of many of the towns stricken by the quake, while those who needed food and shelter the most could not reach safe havens. With more than 2 million people left homeless, experts feared an ongoing catastrophe of mass starvation and disease might kill hundreds of thousands.

> **❝** Like its glorious precedents in New York, Washington and Madrid, the blessed conquest [in Britain] took the battle to the enemy's land. **❞**
>
> **—AYMAN AL-ZAWAHIRI,**
> *al-Qaeda's No.2, on July's bombings in Britain*

The Leaderboard

Voters chose new faces to run Iran and Germany, while the U.N. faced scandals. Not shown here: voters in France and the Netherlands rejected the proposed constitution for the European Union, raising concern about the future of the E.U.

ANGELA MERKEL, GERMANY
After seven years in power, Gerhard Schröder's government fell after a tie vote in an October election. Angela Merkel, 51, born in East Germany, and her Christian Democrats will lead a coalition government.

KIM JONG IL, NORTH KOREA
The dictator pressed for nuclear power he says will be used peacefully in six-party talks led by China and the U.S. China's President Hu Jintao visited the nation in October.

MAHMOUD AHMADINEJAD, IRAN
The mayor of Tehran, an Islamist and foe of the U.S. and the U.N., was elected President on June 24. Former 1970s U.S. hostages in Iran charged he had been one of their captors.

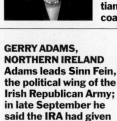

GERRY ADAMS, NORTHERN IRELAND
Adams leads Sinn Fein, the political wing of the Irish Republican Army; in late September he said the IRA had given up its arms, meeting a key goal of the 1998 accord that has calmed the nation's "Troubles"

KOFI ANNAN, UNITED NATIONS
The Secretary-General lost clout when investigators issued a report detailing his son Kojo's connection to payoff scandals in the U.N.'s oil-for-food program in Iraq.

CLOCKWISE FROM TOP LEFT: HERBERT KNOSOWSKI—AP/WIDE WORLD; SOUTH KOREAN

A Looming Pandemic?

Since 1997 the deadly H5N1 strain of the avian-flu virus has traveled steadily west across Asia. The virus began killing humans in Southeast Asia in 2003; now experts are concerned that the flu has the potential to become a global pandemic that might claim millions of lives. Above, workers in Romania slaughtered 40,000 birds when the flu first was identified there in October.

Drawing Board

INEXPENSIVE IMPORTS FROM CHINA

YOU SAVE $6.00

PRICE INCREASE DUE TO EXPANDING CHINESE ECONOMY THAT MADE THE SHOES

OIL

YOU GUESSED IT: $6.00

BEATTIE

News-JournalOnline.com
Copley News Service
©05 Daytona Beach News-Journal

Global Terrorism Report

Terrorists respected no borders in 2005, as radical Islamists pursued their deadly agenda around the world. The July 7 bombings in London were carried out by Britons of Muslim descent, while the island of Bali in Indonesia suffered its second major attack in three years. U.S. officials hope that the suicide attacks by Iraqi civilians in Jordan, below, may be a bellwether event, persuading moderate Middle Eastern Muslims to reject terrorism. If true, the reported killing of top al-Qaeda planner Hamza Rabia in Pakistan on Dec. 3 may be a blow to the terrorism web.

BALI

On Oct. 1 a bomb exploded at a restaurant in the popular tourist town of Kuta on the resort island of Bali in Indonesia, the same city hit by a pair of deadly bombings in 2002. Two restaurants at Jimbaran Bay, not far south, were attacked at the same time. The final death toll in the three bombings was 23 (including the bombers), while hundreds were injured. Jakarta has not been able to capture top agents of Jemaah Islamiah, a jihadist group linked to al-Qaeda that is believed to be responsible for all the bombings.

JORDAN

Suicide bombers struck at three hotels in the capital city of Amman on Nov. 9, leaving 60 dead. A fourth bomb failed, but the strikes were the most devastating in Jordan's history. Abu Mousab al-Zarqawi, the Jordanian who runs al-Qaeda's operations in Iraq, claimed his group had organized the mass murders and said the four bombers were Iraqis. At left, Sajida Mubarak al-Rishawi, an Iraqi who confessed to being the fourth bomber, shows her explosives belt.

AFGHANISTAN

Four years after the Taliban's fall, Afghans are restless. The good news: 50% of voters took part in fall parliamentary elections. The bad: warlords are still in power, and the Taliban is back, thanks to fury over disputed reports of U.S. abuse of the Koran that sparked riots, left.

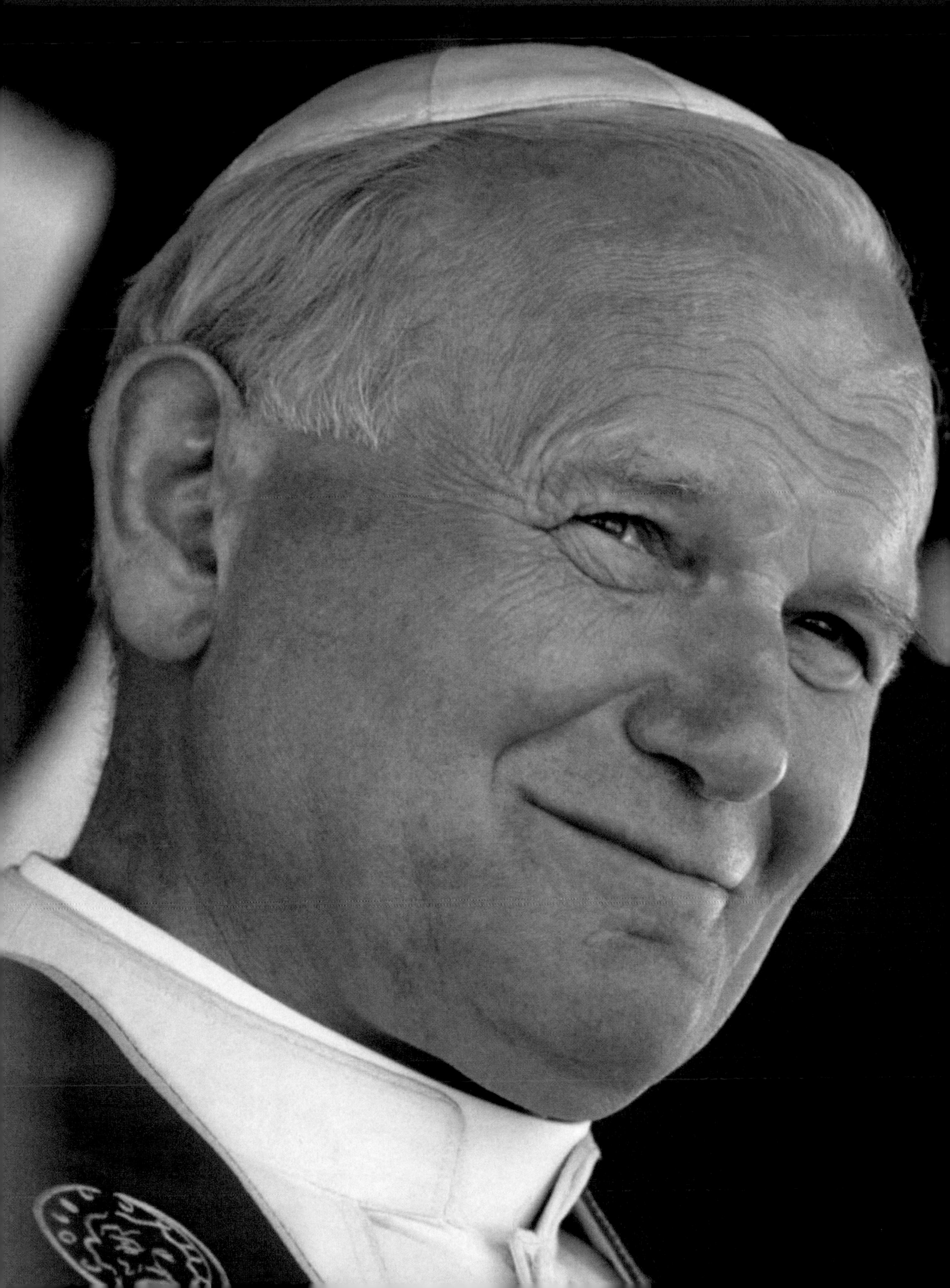

The Bells Toll for A Good Shepherd

As the 26-year reign of Pope John Paul II concludes, the world pauses to honor a man who reshaped his church and his times

BEHOLD: THE SLAVIC POPE IS COMING," WROTE the Polish poet Juliusz Slowacki in 1848, prophetically insisting that a son of Poland would "lead various peoples from darkness into light." The poem was a favorite of Karol Wojtyla's, although the young Pole seems never to have imagined that he would fulfill Slowacki's vision. Yet he did, becoming Pope John Paul II in 1978, and going on to preside over the third longest papacy in history. He became perhaps the greatest emissary to the world the Roman Catholic Church has ever known; helped his native land and its neighbors escape the crushing hand of Soviet hegemony; and steered his church to the right, enforcing conservative stands on such issues as birth control, celibacy and the ordination of women. His power and charisma crossed all lines of creed, nationality, race and age: people everywhere greeted his death on April 2, 2005, as if they had lost a personal spiritual adviser.

Like Ronald Reagan, his ally and fellow great communicator, Wojtyla started out as an actor. His gifts for stirring oratory, apparent even when he was a child, led to his selection as the speaker who would greet distinguished visitors to his secondary school in the grimy industrial town of Wadowice. One visitor, the Archbishop of Cracow, was so impressed by the boy's delivery that he asked what he hoped to do with his life. Told that the teenager was determined to study literature or else pursue a career in acting, the Archbishop answered, "A pity." But he decided to keep an eye on the charismatic young man nonetheless.

That proved crucial, for when Wojtyla finally did take an interest in religious life, he thought himself best suited for a monastery. The young man petitioned the Archbishop three times for permission to join an order of monks. Each time the Archbishop refused. Finally, Wojtyla got the message: he would become a diocesan priest, a shepherd to a flock. By then, deeply Catholic Poland was suffering under Nazi occupation, a national ordeal that would burn into Wojtyla's psyche the strength and presence of evil in this world and cultivate a passionate commitment to resisting it. Forced by the Nazis to work at a limestone quarry, Wojtyla risked his life by attending a secret, illegal school for priests. On at least one occasion, he had to hide in a basement to escape capture by German secret police.

Ordained in 1946, just as a new yoke of oppression, Soviet communism, was being shackled around the neck of his country, the energetic, smart young priest rose rapidly through the hierarchy of his embattled church. In 1958, he became the youngest bishop in Poland. Six years later, he succeeded the man who had guided his early path, the Archbishop of Cracow. Mixing aggressiveness with measured accommodation, Wojtyla defied state atheism and built a huge church for 100,000 Catholic Poles living in the industrial city of Nova Huta; he also reached out to influence a wide cross section of workers, youths and intellectuals. The Second Vatican Council (1961-65) turned a provincial prince into a rising church star: Wojtyla contributed several key documents during the council's deliberations, most notably on the church in the modern world, at one point causing an observer to make note of his "magnetic power" and "prophetic strength."

After Vatican II, Wojtyla was regarded as a protégé of Pope Paul VI's; by 1967 he was a Cardinal. Yet after Paul

YOUTH At age 16, Karol Wojtyla dons native dress for a school play in his hometown of Wadowice

KAYAKER Left, Father Karol Wojtyla enjoys a vacation on a river in Poland. For many years the hearty priest took annual outdoor vacations with a group of old friends and parishioners, many of them married couples

POPE The death of John Paul I after only 34 days in office set the stage for the history-making conclave that elected a non-Italian, Poland's Karol Cardinal Wojtyla, as Pontiff. Below, Wojtyla is invested as Pope John Paul II on Oct. 22, 1978

CAMPER An avid hiker, skier and mountain climber, Wojtyla roughs it in on a trek circa 1960, above. In his first years as Pope, his vigor and power imbued his church with fresh energy

ACTOR The young thespian strikes a pose for a theatrical poster in 1939; during the war, Wojtyla took roles in underground anti-Nazi productions, risking arrest

" Behold: the Slavic Pope is coming/ [To] lead various

died in 1978 and his successor John Paul I succumbed to a heart attack only 34 days into his papacy, Wojtyla was so oblivious to his impending fate that he spent the first day of the new papal conclave browsing through a quarterly review of Marxist theory. When the conclave deadlocked between two leading Italian candidates, a Vatican power broker and an ultraconservative, the Cardinals for the first time since 1522 began looking over the Alps for a leader. Wojtyla was elected on the eighth ballot; at 58, he was the youngest Pope in 132 years.

Almost immediately, John Paul's personal history, his duties as Pontiff and the late 20th century's greatest drama converged in a breathtaking moment. The election of a Polish Pope posed an implicit threat to Poland's Soviet-backed regime, an advantage John Paul quickly exploited with two visits home. His first, in 1979, drew enormous, bloc-shaking crowds; 14 months later, the new Solidarity free-trade-union movement made him its patron saint, flying the papal flag at the gate of the Gdansk shipyard, where it was striking. One month after his next trip, in 1983, Poland's leader, General Wojciech Jaruzelski, lifted the "state of war" he had declared to squash Solidarity.

The journey of the man who had only begun to lead his people from darkness into light was nearly cut short on May 13, 1981. During John Paul II's weekly audience in St. Peter's Square, shots rang out, and he toppled backward, his white cassock stained red. Mehmet Ali Agca, a Turkish rightist and murderer who had earlier written a letter vowing to kill the Pope, had tried to make good on his threat. Doctors removed part of the Pope's intestine; he had lost so much blood that almost all of it was replaced by transfusions. Agca's motives remain shrouded: many investigators suspect he was aided by Eastern-bloc intelligence services that wished to be rid of Solidarity's patron.

But John Paul II—who visited Agca's prison cell in 1983 and, in a stunning gesture, forgave him—would not be deterred from his goal. For the next few years, the Pope adroitly balanced his role as the champion of Poland's liberation with his resolve that his nation's freedom would be achieved without violence. By serving as a catalyst and mediator in the peaceful toppling of Warsaw's communist regime in 1989, he performed what can be described, without exaggeration, as a miracle.

This most ecumenical of Popes traveled relentlessly,

PILGRIM Fulfilling a longtime dream, John Paul visited the Holy Land in 2000, meeting with both Muslim and Jewish leaders. In Jerusalem, he stopped to place a prayer at the Western Wall, right

MOURNER The Pope visited the Nazi death camp at Auschwitz, Poland, in 1979, left; in a 1998 encyclical, John Paul acknowledged that the church had failed to take a forceful stand against the Nazis

ALLY Below, John Paul visits with Mother Teresa in 1986 in Calcutta. After her death, he put the icon of charity on a fast track for sainthood

CONFESSOR Turkish agitator Mehmet Ali Agca shot the Pope in St. Peter's Square in 1981; two years later John Paul came to Agca's jail cell, prayed with his assailant and forgave him

IMAGES: AFP—GETTY IMAGES; BETTMANN CORBIS; GIANNI GIANSANTI—CORBIS

peoples from darkness into light." —Juliusz Slowacki

taking his message (and charisma) to the world and reaching out to other faiths. In 1986, he gathered an extraordinary spectrum of religious leaders, from the Dalai Lama and the Archbishop of Canterbury to Sikh clerics and Zoroastrian priests, in the Italian town of Assisi, where they prayed together. He was the first Pope to visit a mosque and the first modern Pontiff to enter a synagogue.

Seeking to cleanse his church in preparation for the millennium, John Paul II squarely faced the darker moments in Catholic history. He issued apologies for both the Inquisition and the Crusades and rehabilitated Galileo for the "heresy" of espousing the theory that the sun was the center of the solar system. In 1998 he released the encyclical letter "We Remember," an acknowledgment of the church's failure to grapple with the Nazi Holocaust.

But this spirit of reconciliation did not extend to matters of doctrine, where the Pope reaffirmed a wide range of conservative teachings on birth control, the ordination of women, priestly celibacy and homosexuality. He rebuffed priests advocating liberation theology in the Americas, silenced theologians who questioned church orthodoxy and let the sex-abuse scandals in the American church fester

for too long before addressing them. Attuned to Catholicism's mystical aspects, he canonized an astonishing 482 saints, more than all his predecessors combined; he was especially devoted to the Virgin Mary.

John Paul's increasingly frail health in the twilight of his papacy caused many to wonder if he would become the first Pope in 590 years to retire. Instead, he chose to make his life another kind of example, showing a world obsessed with youth that illness and old age are not badges of shame. From a wheelchair, he gave audience after audience and celebrated Mass after public Mass.

Yet even this great spirit could not endure forever. On Saturday, April 2, John Paul II uttered his final halting words. "You have come to me," he said, "and I thank you." Whether the 84-year-old was talking to the circle of priests around him, the thousands of pilgrims standing vigil outside his window or the waiting Lord above, there was no way to know. A few minutes later, the man who had made history itself kneel down was gone. Within an hour, the bells began tolling over St. Peter's Square, and around the world, people of all faiths paused to offer prayers for that rarest of wonders, a Slavic Pope. ∎

POLAND **1979**   DEPARTING ARGENTINA **1982**   AFRICA **1980**   MONT BLANC 19

■ Pilgrim's Progress

ONCE UPON A TIME IN THE CATHOLIC CHURCH, ALL roads led to Rome: pilgrims from every land came to the Vatican, hoping to catch a glimpse of the Pope blessing the crowd from a faraway balcony at St. Peter's Square. A privileged few might be invited to an audience with the Pontiff. But to generations of the faithful, the Pope was a distant figure, shrouded in mystery and incense, remote and unknowable.

John Paul 11 had a better idea: in his papacy, he seemed to take every road he could find *away* from Rome, bringing his message—and his matchless charisma—directly to his flock. The sheer record of his travels is exhausting: in his 26 years as Pope, John Paul traveled some 800,000 miles and visited more than 125 countries. All those pilgrimages were memorable, and some of them made history. His first visit to Poland, in 1979, rallied his countrymen, uniting them in opposition to their Soviet-dominated government; he returned in 1983 to lend his support to the Solidarity free-trade-union movement. The nationwide reaction to his first visit to the U.S., in 1979, was so memorable that TIME put the Pope's picture on the cover over the headline JOHN PAUL, SUPERSTAR.

John Paul traveled as an evangelist but also as an ecumenist, reaching out to other faiths as no other Pontiff had before him. He was the first modern Pope to visit a synagogue, the first to enter a mosque, the first to visit the Holy

PORTUGAL 1991

GUATEMALA 1983

GIANSANTI—CORBIS–GAMMA, FELLICH—GAMMA, ANTICOLI LIVIO—LIUSA—GAMMA, FRANÇOIS LOCHON—GAMMA

Land. He became the first Pope to visit Greece in 13 centuries, but he failed to attain one of his greatest goals, a reconciliation with the Orthodox branch of the church. John Paul visited places of hope and healing, Catholic shrines such as Fatima and Lourdes (his final major pilgrimage, in the summer of 2004). He visited places of great evil: Auschwitz and Babi Yar, near Kiev in Ukraine, scene of a horrendous World War II massacre. In sum, this energetic pilgrim remade his church; under John Paul it became less Roman—and more catholic.

Even St. Paul, the archetypal evangelist, might have wondered at John Paul's 1989, a fairly typical year: it featured stops in Madagascar, Réunion, Zambia, Malawi,

Norway, Iceland, Finland, Denmark, Sweden, Spain, South Korea, Indonesia, East Timor and Mauritius. Over time, a ritual of arrival was developed: the Pope would land at each destination and kiss the airport tarmac. With his square jaw, actor's timing and facility with languages, he established a personal connection with tens of millions of people, especially young people, with whom he shared a special bond. One impressed witness was a Protestant minister who attended the Pope's Mass in a vast field at the Living History Farms in Iowa during John Paul's first U.S. visit. After watching the Pontiff's electrifying effect on the huge crowd, the minister turned to his neighbor, a farmer, and said, "You got a Pope who knows how to pope." ■

VENEZUELA 1986

■ A Funeral, a Conclave and *"Habemus Papam!"*

THEODORE CARDINAL MCCARRICK OF WASHINGTON called it "the largest funeral in the history of the world," and few observers disagreed. For several weeks in April, the world's eyes and thoughts were trained on Vatican City in Rome, as the extraordinary spectacle of Pope John Paul II's funeral and the election of his successor played out in vivid contrasts of sorrow and elation.

The faithful who clogged Rome's streets and the tens of millions around the world watching on television, Roman Catholic and non-Catholic alike, knew that they were honoring a man who had helped shape history. The reverberations of John Paul's life and pontificate, the third longest in history, had resounded through every nation on earth. His deeds and example helped topple a superpower, bringing freedom to hundreds of millions of people. They reaffirmed the Catholic message of salvation to millions more, often in nations never before touched by Rome. They resonated in synagogues and mosques, and they made the Slavic Pope's own church rattle and hum.

In the end, not every Catholic—and certainly not every American Catholic—considered John Paul's reign an entirely joyful noise unto the Lord. But the 264th occupant of the throne of St. Peter had been no more silenced by their misgivings than he had been by the would-be assassin's bullet he survived in 1981 or the progressive ailments, including Parkinson's disease, that he withstood so bravely for at least a decade. The world knew it was honoring a man who had pursued God's truth with a fearless, anachronistic, nearly stunning purity of purpose; now that great spirit had been stilled.

The population of Rome doubled in a matter of days, as millions of the faithful and the curious made the pilgrimage to the Eternal City, including 2 million Poles who came to honor their native son. There was no room at any inn, so people camped in the streets and squares while the city tested its gift for hospitality. Romans were urged to open their doors, take people in. The government set up thousands of cots in soccer stadiums, the convention center and makeshift tent cities; handed out bottles of water and blankets and pillows that had been stockpiled in anticipation of the eruption of Mount Vesuvius.

If the visitors brought nothing else, they brought cell phones, and it made for a thoroughly modern mourning. The Italian Civil Protection Agency sent out text messages advising people when the line would be closed, although warnings of a 15-hour wait to view the Pope's casket, displayed in St. Peter's Square, did not seem to discourage people. When night fell, the great basilica glimmered, and still they came, intent on seeing him one last time. As many as 18,000 people passed by every hour, moving almost too fast to pray. The cell phones served as cameras, capturing a digital relic to carry home.

By Friday, April 8, when the Princes and Presidents, Kings and Queens, Metropolitans and Patriarchs had all arrived to honor their brother, the world seemed to stop to say Mass. In the shadow of John Paul's passing, much history was laid to rest; the church's strengths and weaknesses were also laid out for all to see. Here was Prince Charles, in line to lead an Anglican Church that split with Rome over a King's divorce five centuries ago: the Prince had postponed his wedding a day to attend this ceremony instead. There was Boston's Bernard Cardinal Law, now in Rome after resigning over his handling of the sex-abuse scandals, preparing to preside over one of the week's funeral Masses. There were representatives of the Arab League, the King of Jordan, the Palestinian Prime Minister, the President of Syria, come from lands where the memory of the Crusades still rankles. Here was the President of the U.S. seated near the President of Iran, and all the heads of the world, friends and enemies laced together in liturgy, sharing, at least for this moment, a sign of peace.

Outside the square, the multitudes watched, on immense TV screens, the movement of the plain cypress coffin, a fitting last gesture by a Pope who understood so well how much images matter. Banners proclaimed, SANTO SUBITO (Sainthood Now). Then it was over, and by late afternoon the young pilgrims broke out coolers of soft drinks, packed the cafés, strolled down to the Tiber River. Grief had turned festive with the echo of what the Pope on his deathbed is said to have told his personal secretary: "I am happy," he said. "You be happy too." Romans took a deep breath and turned their eyes from the past to the future, for the shoes of this great fisherman were now to be filled, as the electors of the College of Cardinals gathered for the first papal conclave in more than a quarter-century.

FINAL JOURNEY: On April 4, two days after his death, the body of Pope John Paul II was borne into the Basilica of St. Peter's, where it would lie in state as millions passed by

MASSIMO SAMBUCETTI-AP/WIDE WORLD

NINE DAYS LATER, THE ELECTORS, 117 STRONG, FILED into the Sistine Chapel to begin the conclave. And two days after that, as crowds milled in St. Peter's Square, smoke began to pour from the chapel's tin chimney for the fourth time, the signal that a fourth ballot had been taken. Inside, the Cardinals were wrestling with the stove in the corner just left of the entrance. "They were trying to get enough chemicals on the fire to make the smoke white," Chicago's Francis Cardinal George later re-

called. "The stove backed up, pouring smoke into the chapel." Outside, when the first tendrils appeared, they were gray and vague. But in time they whitened, and then the bells pealed, and people came running into the square to hear the news: "*Habemus Papam!*" We have a Pope!

A wave of welcome came washing over the small man who now stepped out onto the balcony. "*Viva il Papa!*" the crowd chanted as they got a first sight of the new Pontiff. Joseph Cardinal Ratzinger of Germany—now Pope Bene-

dict XVI—raised his hands and circled his arms, like a large bird at lift-off. Typical Pope behavior, but not typical of Ratzinger. "You know, we believe grace comes with the office," said Cardinal George. "When he came out on the balcony and started waving his arms, I thought, 'It's working! I've never seen him make those gestures before!' "

The choice of Cardinal Ratzinger surprised many: he had served as John Paul's theological watchdog since 1981, earning the nickname "God's Rottweiler" and a reputation as a tough, autocratic conservative. The *Sun* of London would headline his bio FROM HITLER YOUTH TO PAPA RATZI. But Ratzinger's election came as no surprise to a tight inner circle of conservative Cardinals in the Vatican Curia, who had begun a stealth campaign to transfigure a candidate long considered unpalatable into an inevitable Pontiff 18 months before the conclave began. The late Pope had done his part over the years, naming 115 of the 117 Cardinals eligible to vote, stacking the college with men likely to want to continue his conservative policies. Just as important, most of the influential Cardinals of liberal stripe had passed the voting-age limit of 80.

The only prelate of sufficient stature left to rally wavering Cardinals to the liberal cause was Carlo Maria Cardinal Martini of Milan. But after Martini, a biblical scholar, had gone off to study in Jerusalem in 2002, Ratzinger began running an effective campaign to win friends in Italy and the Curia. The effort paid off when Ratzinger led the first ballot in the conclave, then gradually picked up votes, easily winning election on the fourth ballot.

In Ratzinger, the conclave chose a figure who will serve as both a continuation of John Paul II's legacy and a bridge to whatever will follow it. By picking a traditional-

MOURNING At top, pilgrims gather in front of St. Peter's Basilica to view John Paul's body; above, St. Peter's Square is filled to capacity during the funeral; left, a scene in Wadowice, where the future Pope was born in 1920

ist, the Cardinals got continuity; by choosing an experienced manager, they restored administrative discipline; with a 78-year-old in uncertain health (Ratzinger suffered a cerebral hemorrhage in 1991), they got, in effect, a transitional figure. And they got a man prepared to lead: when Jorge Cardinal Arturo Medina Estevez—who would announce the election from the balcony of St. Peter's—asked Ratzinger what name he would assume, the Pontiff-elect did not hesitate. "In the past, there's been a wait while the new Pope pondered the question for 10 minutes or so," an informed source told TIME after the conclave. "Not so this time. Ratzinger replied right away, 'Benedict XVI.' He was prepared." ■

A Right Turn on the Long Road to the Papacy

POPE BENEDICT XVI WAS BORN JOSEPH ALOYSIUS Ratzinger on Holy Saturday—April 16, 1927—into a devout Catholic family in southern Bavaria. His father, a police officer, attended three Masses every Sunday; after the Nazis came to power, he was demoted for predicting that a victory by Hitler would bring on the Apocalypse. Like many Bavarians, the Ratzingers became anti-Nazi, if not heroically so, after Hitler began voicing anti-Catholic sentiments. Although much has been made of the new Pope's having once belonged to the Hitler Youth, such membership was compulsory, and Ratzinger's involvement appears to have been brief and unenthusiastic. His military service seems to have been similar. In a 1993 interview with TIME, he explained that although he was drafted into the paramilitary corps in 1943, an infected finger prevented him from learning how to shoot. The following year he put up tank traps near the borders of Czechoslovakia, Austria and Hungary, where, he recalled in the same interview, he saw Hungarian Jews being shipped to their death. At war's end, he did some time in a U.S. POW camp, then made his way home to Bavaria.

"The abyss of Hitlerism could not be overlooked," he would later recall, and the depravities of the Nazis led to the young Ratzinger's conviction that religion was crucial to civilization. His profound suspicion of human judgment and secular authority echo in his memory of the Latin Mass he loved as a child: "Here I was encountering a reality that no one had simply thought up, a reality that no official authority or great individual had created. It was much more than a product of human history."

In 1951, Ratzinger followed his older brother Georg into the priesthood. Quickly recognized as a talented theological thinker, Ratzinger raced through a series of appointments at prestigious German universities, developing a reputation as a liberal reformer. In 1962, at only 35, he was honored with an invitation to attend the Second Vatican Council as a theological adviser. While there, he wrote speeches criticizing the Inquisition and calling for greater openness in church teaching. After Vatican II he was appointed theology dean of the University of Tübingen.

The year 1968, which saw massive college protests in Germany, seems to have been a turning point for Ratzinger. Like other German universities, Tübingen became a hotbed of radical theology. Students distributed flyers calling the crucifix a sadomasochistic artifact. They threw tomatoes and yanked away professors' microphones to disrupt lectures and force "dialogue."

"Those were tough times," recalled theologian Hans Küng, who was, up to that time, Ratzinger's partner in calling for greater openness in church teaching. "And Ratzinger did not digest them very well." Wolfgang Beinert, a student of Ratzinger's at Tübingen, remembers that the rebellion "had an extraordinarily strong impact" on the future Pope: "Suddenly he saw these new ideas were connected to violence and a destruction of the order ... He was simply no longer able to bear it."

BLESSING **The new Pope salutes his flock**

As a newly minted conservative, Ratzinger voiced reservations about the church's leftward drift after Vatican II and warned against accepting "tenets merely because they happen to be fashionable at the moment." In 1977, he was named Archbishop of Munich by Pope Paul VI. Soon afterward, Ratzinger cultivated an alliance with a fellow Cardinal who shared his view of the church as the bulwark against barbaric atheism and dehumanizing secularism: Karol Wojtyla, the Archbishop of Cracow and the future John Paul II. In 1981, three years after his accession, John Paul invited Ratzinger to join him in Rome. The Pope installed the German Cardinal as chief of the Congregation for the Doctrine of the Faith (the new name given to the office Ratzinger had once criticized, the Inquisition), making him the church's doctrinal enforcer. "God's Rottweiler" used his office to silence scores of dissident theologians around the world—not least among them, his onetime friend and colleague, Hans Küng. But Ratzinger saw his work as instructing Catholics on both the proper way—and the forbidden way. "I think there is an obligation to protect people," he told TIME in 1993, "to help them to see this [doctrinal error] is not our faith." Now, after decades of playing the Vatican's "Dr. No," Benedict XVI will face a new challenge: learning to accentuate the positive. ■

Society

LOST IN THE WHIRLWIND

The debate over whether to remove the feeding tube sustaining the life of Terri Schiavo, the comatose Florida woman whose brain had been seriously damaged since 1990, involved serious ethical issues. But when the case became an excuse for posturing on all sides of the political spectrum, the sad plight of the woman at the center of the frenzy seemed to have become a sideshow. When federal legislators tried to intervene, many Americans recoiled: in a TIME poll taken in late March, three-quarters of the respondents declared the woman's fate was a private family matter.

CARLOS BARRIA—REUTERS—CORBIS

The Rev. Billy Graham

WHEN 86-YEAR-OLD BILLY GRAHAM SPOKE TO A CROWD of some 90,000 people in New York City's Flushing Meadows Park on June 26, his aides insisted that his remarks had been the final sermon of his final crusade in America. But while the legendary preacher's flesh was far weaker than it had been in his vigorous prime, when TIME dubbed him "God's machine-gun"—he suffers from Parkinson's disease, water on the brain and several other ailments—his spirit was willing. "Never say never," he declared. "Never is a bad word, because we never know."

In his 25-minute sermon, Graham spoke of last things, citing the travails of the world as evidence that the apoca-lypse is at hand. And he saluted his longtime vocalist, George Beverly Shea, 96, saying: "I know that it won't be long before both of us are going to be in heaven." When that day arrives, the Rev. Graham will have quite a story to tell St. Peter: the three-day gathering in New York City was his 417th crusade, and the Graham organization estimates that its leader has spoken live to more than 83 million people since he first began evangelizing in the late 1940s. As Graham preached, his son Franklin stood by, ready to take his father's place should the patriarch falter. But Franklin's help wasn't needed; and besides, as his son would be the first to admit, Billy Graham is irreplaceable. ■

Edgar Ray Killen

MIGHTY LONG TIME," IS HOW FANNIE LEE CHANEY—whose son, civil-rights worker James Chaney, was slain by the Ku Klux Klan in 1964—summed up her feelings about the January 2005 indictment of Mississippi Klan leader Edgar Ray Killen for her son's murder. Killen, known to Neshoba County locals as "the Preacher," called himself a Baptist minister, but he worshiped at the altar of hate. When he became his local Klan's Kleagle (leader) in the early 1960s, Killen, ordained with power, enlisted more than a dozen Klansmen who conspired in the murder of Chaney and fellow activists Andrew Goodman and Michael Schwerner. The killings appalled most Americans and inspired the 1988 film *Mississippi Burning*. But Killen and his fellow Klansmen had never faced state murder charges. Indeed, 11 of 18 suspects (including Killen), had been acquitted on charges of federal civil-rights violations in a 1967 trial. One member of the all-white jury later said that she could never convict a man of God like Killen.

But the South has changed. By 2005, support for Killen had evaporated in Mississippi: in one poll almost 70% of respondents supported his arrest. When a new investigation, triggered by a series of articles in a local newspaper, led to Killen's indictment and trial, a racially mixed jury took less than six hours to find him guilty on three counts of manslaughter. Killen, 80, was sentenced to the maximum of 60 years in prison. After the verdict, Andrew Goodman's mother, Carolyn, 89, reflected that if she were able to confront Killen, "I would ask him what was on his mind" that night, but then added, "Could he tell me? Would it help him any?"

Steve Wynn

L AS VEGAS IS NO PLACE FOR SMALL GESTURES, SO IT WAS entirely appropriate that when veteran hotelier Steve Wynn completed his new $2.7 billion resort on the famed Strip, he would not only give it his name but also top it off with his scrawled autograph. In fact, Wynn's signature is all over modern-day Vegas, which has enjoyed a roaring revival since the mogul, 63, began hauling the old gambling city into the modern era with such over-the-top hotels as 1989's Mirage (fronted by a fake volcano), 1993's Treasure Island (fronted by a fake pirate show) and 1998's Bellagio (fronted by a real $40 million fountain and home to museum-quality art). Wynn Disneyfied Vegas, turning a city that was a pit stop for male vice into a family attraction, cramming roulette and Renoirs under the same roof.

For his next act, Wynn hopes to up the ante on Vegas luxury by pulling back a notch. Influenced by his wife Elaine's interest in Buddhism, Wynn met the Dalai Lama and pro-

fesses to have discovered the joys of restraint. Mind you, restraint for Wynn translates into a resort boasting an eight-story, pine-covered mountain with cascading waterfalls; an in-house Ferrari dealership; 2,716 rooms; 18 restaurants; and 31 stores. "This is the most understated overstated hotel in the world," Wynn told TIME, and indeed the resort's low ceilings, short hallways and ample nooks give it an intimate feel. And for that final, restrained touch, look under your sheets: every mattress bears the signature of you-know-who. ∎

Carly Fiorina

FOR YEARS, CARLY FIORINA PROSPERED FROM THE OUTSIZE image she projected: few of the hundreds of stories written about her failed to describe her as the "rock star of the computer world." The articulate, energetic CEO of Hewlett-Packard was indeed a Bono of bytes, from her tailored clothing to her Gulfstream jet. But when she couldn't generate a bottom line that matched her high profile, the HP board unceremoniously dismissed her in February.

It was a rough ending for the brilliant salesperson who did many things right after she was hired from Lucent to give the stumbling computer giant an overhaul in 1999. Asked to create a strategic vision for a company that had none, she came up with dazzling insights into "transfor-mational trends" and a hyperdigital future in which HP would serve consumers and corporations at every stage. She streamlined HP's ramshackle structure and, in her most controversial move, led the $19 billion acquisition of rival Compaq in 2002. Yet Fiorina couldn't make the Compaq gambit pay off, and when the HP board began to regard her self-confidence as hubris—well, live by the sword, die by the board. Count Fiorina, 51, as down but not out. "Have I taken risks through my whole life? Yes," she told TIME in 2002. "The risk that is not worth taking is to do the easy thing and do nothing." The notion of this driven visionary doing nothing simply doesn't compute. Look for Fiorina to take a few more risks before her story wraps. ■

PRO/CON: Demonstrators on both sides rallied for weeks in Florida

FIGHT TO THE FINISH

As Americans battle over a woman's right to live or die, Terri Schiavo's plight is almost eclipsed by rhetoric, protests and political posturing

AMERICANS FOUND MUCH TO DISAGREE about in 2005: among them, the war in Iraq, the handling of Hurricane Katrina and the theory of evolution. Yet perhaps the single most divisive issue in the quarrelsome Republic was the fate of a 41-year-old Florida woman who had lingered for 15 years in a twilight state beyond consciousness. Around this woman an unseemly dance of death unfolded as her room in a heavily guarded hospice in Pinellas Park became the latest front in America's ongoing cultural wars.

How did it come to this? On Feb. 25, 1990, 26-year-old Terri Schiavo went into cardiac arrest, the result of a potassium imbalance that may have been caused by an eating disorder. Deprived of oxygen for more than five minutes while she was transported to the hospital and resuscitated, her brain was seriously damaged and she slipped into a coma. The hopes of husband Michael and parents Robert and Mary Schindler that Terri might recover rallied briefly in May, when her eyes opened and she resumed waking and sleeping cycles. But the extent of the damage to Terri's brain also started to become apparent. Although she was not brain dead (that condition occurs when there is no activity anywhere in the brain), she demonstrated no awareness of herself or her surroundings. She retained enough brain function to breath and pump blood on her own and perform certain reflex actions (like blinking her eyes), but doctors found no evidence of activity in her cerebral cortex, the

LIVELY: Terri Schiavo before her collapse in 1990

thinking part of the brain. That is what doctors call a vegetative state, and when it continues for more than a month without any sign of improvement, the diagnosis may be changed to persistent vegetative state (PVS). In the months and years that followed Terri's cardiac arrest, several teams of doctors all characterized Terri's condition as irreversible PVS.

Still, for more than three years, the Schiavo family waited for some sign of improvement in Terri's condition. When none materialized, her husband, who had been appointed his wife's legal guardian after the 1990 illness, concluded that there was no realistic hope of Terri's recovery. Insisting that his wife, who had not made out a living will, had previously told him she did not want to be kept alive in an incapacitated state, he authorized a 1994 do-not-resuscitate order in case of another heart attack. Four years later, he petitioned a Florida court for the removal of Terri's feeding tube. The Schindler family—devout Catholics who had fallen out with Michael over their daughter's treatment and the distribution of money he was awarded when he successfully sued a doctor for malpractice in the case—strongly opposed removal of the life-giving tube.

A gruesome period followed: twice between 2000 and 2003, Terri's feeding tube was removed by a judge's order; twice the Schindlers succeeded in getting it put back; twice the U.S. Supreme Court refused to review lower-court orders in favor of removal. The second time the tube was dis-

connected, on Oct. 15, 2003, the Schindlers filed a federal suit and appealed to pro-life groups for support.

Enter the politicians, attracted to the case as it became a rallying point for pro-life advocates, who viewed the removal of the feeding tube as murder. Schiavo's fate was becoming a cause célèbre, not just for those fighting the right-to-die movement but also in the nation's larger ongoing battles over abortion, stem-cell research and judicial activism. In 2004 the Florida legislature hastily passed "Terri's Law" to allow Governor Jeb Bush to order the tube reinserted. Now it was Michael's turn to sue. In May 2004, Florida state Judge W. Douglas Baird ruled that Terri's Law was unconstitutional, a decision later upheld by the Florida Supreme Court; the U.S. Supreme Court again refused to get involved.

On March 18, 2005, while the Florida legislature tried (unsuccessfully) to draft a new law to intercede, state Judge George Greer ordered the feeding tube disconnected once again. By now, Terri's fate was preoccupying the nation: leading the news, sparking public rallies, dominating blogs and websites. That day, the House of Representatives, led by Republican majority leader Tom DeLay, took the extraordinary step of issuing a subpoena ordering Schiavo herself to appear before Congress, along with her doctors and family. The move was rebuffed by Judge Greer, who said there was "no cogent reason" for Congress to intervene. In the hours after her feeding tube was removed, the G.O.P.-controlled House and Senate convened a special session—in the midst of Congress's Easter recess—to craft a measure transferring jurisdiction in the case to the federal courts.

During the debate, DeLay described the removal of Terri's feeding tube as an "act of medical terrorism," while Senate majority leader Bill Frist, a physician, defied years of reports by doctors on the scene and declared on the Senate floor that "there seems to be insufficient information to conclude that Terry Schiavo is in a persistent vegetative state." Three days later, President Bush conspicuously interrupted a vacation and dramatically returned to Washington to sign Congress's bill at 1:11 a.m.—although he

could have done so at his Texas ranch. For the next week, the Schindlers filed repeated appeals in state and federal courts; all of them were denied.

All but drowned out amid this circus was Michael Schiavo's insistence that all he wanted for his wife was a dignified death. And despite the bluster, most Americans—even those who described themselves as born-again or evangelical Christians—supported the decision to remove Terri Schiavo's feeding tube. In a TIME poll, fully three-quarters of respondents (including 68% of Republicans) said it was wrong for Congress to intervene in the matter, and two-thirds said they believed that the actions in Washington were rooted more in politics than principles.

FINALLY, AT 9:05 AM ON MARCH 31, 14 DAYS AFTER HER feeding tube had been removed for the last time, Terri Schiavo died. An autopsy later revealed that in the years of her ordeal, her brain had shrunk to half its normal size, and she had gone blind. She was, in short, never going to get better.

On the simple headstone that adorns Terri's grave, Michael Schiavo inscribed the words, I KEPT MY PROMISE. The sentiment further inflamed his detractors, who say the relationship he maintains with a woman with whom he had two children following his wife's physical decline is further evidence of his moral failings. But most Americans seemed to reject the notion that there could be any winners in this ugly and tragic family spectacle.

Beyond the heart-wrenching specifics of the case, the Schiavo controversy raised important questions about the Federal Government's encroaching on states' rights, individual rights and the judiciary, not to mention the role religion should play in politics and the legal system. Most of all, though, Terri Schiavo's lamentable fate compelled many people to think seriously about what it means to be alive or dead, and how they might prepare for their own death. In the wake of a single fatality, tens of thousands of Americans began making out living wills and appointing health-care proxies—one blessing in a case so filled with religious imagery yet so devoid of grace. ∎

Above, Florida Governor Jeb Bush meets with Terri Schiavo's mother Mary Schindler; husband Robert and sister Suzanne, at rear; and brother Bobby, on the right. Michael Schiavo, left, had his late wife's ashes interred without notifying her family of the event

RIGHT, TOP: STEVE NESIUS—AP/WIDE WORLD. BOTTOM: PRESTON MACK—ZUMA PRESS

CIRCUS **Jackson's supporters came from around the world to defend their hero's integrity; media came from around the world to chronicle the latest chapter in the once dazzling pop star's ongoing decline**

D.A. STALKS

JURY BALKS

MICHAEL WALKS

WORLD GAWKS

JACKO TO SNEDDON:

BEAT IT!

MAYBE IT WASN'T QUITE O.J. ALL OVER AGAIN, BUT THE 2005 trial of fading pop star Michael Jackson on charges that he had molested a 15-year-old boy at his lavish Neverland Ranch in California still served up heaping doses of salaciousness—and came to a similar verdict. The only beneficiaries of the 14-week exercise were the same vultures who had feasted on the O.J. Simpson show trial back in the day: America's ever expanding casbah of celebrity-fixated TV shows, tabloids and websites, each of which demands a regular diet of titillating stories to feed its maw. Any story involving "Wacko Jacko," now 46 (going on 16), is catnip for this crowd.

In this case, it was just what the D.A. ordered. Santa Barbara County prosecutor Tom Sneddon had been itching to nail the Gloved One since he failed to do so in an aborted 1993 molestation trial. Jackson strayed into his sights again with the February 2003 U.S. broadcast of a documentary, first aired on British television, in which the star acknowledged sharing his bed with boys and described the practice, which he called "a beautiful thing," as a way of showing his love for children. Appearing onscreen with Jackson was a young cancer patient, then 13, who was shown holding hands with Jackson and cuddling beside him on a couch. After watching the broadcast, an infuriated Sneddon opened a new criminal investigation into Jackson's behavior.

Jackson and his entourage—never accused of embracing reality too tightly—somehow had imagined that the documentary would burnish the star's image, but they quickly realized that it amounted to a public-relations meltdown. In a frantic attempt at damage control, they decided to produce a rebuttal documentary and for this reason invited the boy and his brother back to Neverland. While there, both children spent the night in Jackson's bedroom.

"I was under the covers, and that is when he put his hand down my pants and started masturbating me," Jackson's accuser, now 15, would testify in March. Later, during the same visit, he recalled, "he did it one more time." He said that Jackson also showed him and his younger brother pornography in magazines and on the Internet, and plied them with wine—"Jesus juice," he said Jackson called it—in Diet Coke cans.

Jackson's defense team was led by Thomas Mesereau, an A-list Los Angeles criminal lawyer whose needling cross-examinations at times irritated Judge Rodney Melville but often scored points. Mesereau got the accuser's sister to backtrack on key testimony, and turned another witness, former Jackson crisis-control expert Ann Marie Kite, into a voice for the defense. He provoked the boy's mother into alienating the jury with rambling, incoherent and argumentative testimony that left her credibility in tatters. ("I was acting," she said dismissively, after being confronted with a videotape in which she and her children lavishly praised Jackson for helping the family.)

Throughout the trial, Mesereau sowed seeds of doubt as to whether the boy's family, whom he called "con artists, actors and liars," was trying to do anything more than shake Jackson down for money. (The star had previously paid out millions of dollars to settle civil claims arising from accusations of child molestation; the accuser's family had previously received a $152,000 settlement from J.C. Penney after the mother accused store security guards of groping her.) And Mesereau marshaled a parade of Hollywood stars, including comics Jay Leno and Chris Tucker, to vouch for Jackson's character.

More than once, Mesereau's work was complicated by his client. Jackson repeatedly arrived late to court and once showed up hobbling and wearing pajama bottoms as trousers. Prosecutors reveled in the picture that the defendant seemed to be painting for them: a faded star (Jackson has not had a No. 1 hit since *You Are Not Alone*, in 1995) who has allowed surgeons to ravage his face until he bears a closer resemblance to the Phantom of the Opera than his beloved Peter Pan. Now famous primarily for being notorious, Jackson is not the first celebrity to be so hypnotized by the limelight that he pampers his quirks instead of developing his work, nor the only one to remain addicted to the high life long after the big money ebbed.

But Jackson was not on trial for his eccentricity. In the end, jurors had to decide whom to believe: the accuser, who is a child, or the accused, who seems to think he still is. On June 13, after 30 hours of deliberation, they chose the latter, acquitting Jackson of each one of the 10 charges against him. In an unusual twist, the verdict left the losing side unbowed, while chastening the winners. Prosecutor Sneddon said, "I'm not going to look back and apologize for anything we've done," and he snapped "no comment," when asked if he thought a child molester had gone free. As for Jackson, a member of his legal team announced that the star has decided to abandon the practice of sharing his bed with young boys. ∎

AMPERSANDS 2005

Let's see: Tom and Katie, Brad and Angelina … Hillary and Newt? Our annual survey of the year's most gossipworthy get-togethers

DANNY MOLOSHO<—AP/WIDE WORLD (2)

BRAD & ANGELINA: Nice guy Brad Pitt and *Good Girl* Jennifer Aniston became one of America's favorite couples after their 2000 wedding. But the pair announced they would split in January, after Pitt co-starred with slinky Angelina Jolie in a 60-plus-page *W Magazine* photo shoot promoting their thriller flick *Mr. and Mrs. Smith.* Despite initial protests that there was no spark between them, the two began traveling together, and Jolie moved into Pitt's Malibu home in July. Said Aniston of her ex: "[With Brad] there's a sensitivity chip that's missing."

TOM & KATIE: Tom Cruise's long ride as one of Hollywood's seemingly more stable stars ended in 2005, when the twice-divorced actor, still boyish at 43, seemed to go haywire over new flame Katie Holmes, 27. His infatuation, nicely timed to coincide with the promotional priorities of their summer movies *War of the Worlds* and *Batman Begins,* took several startling forms. A flamboyant Cruise proposed at the top of the Eiffel Tower; mounted the couch on Oprah Winfrey's TV show, left, to act out his passion; then directed outright ridicule at NBC's *Today Show* anchor Matt Lauer on the subject of psychiatry, which is regarded as a pseudo-science by Cruise and his fellow Scientologists.

CHARLES & CAMILLA After 35 years of courtship, which spanned a pair of marriages that ended in divorce, Prince Charles, 56, heir to the British throne, finally married his paramour, Lady Camilla Parker Bowles, 57. The marriage, which was delayed a day as Charles attended the funeral of Pope John Paul II, took place in the town hall in Windsor, England.

RENEE & KENNY Much loved Hollywood star Renée Zellweger, 36, got in touch with her Texas-girl roots this year; she tied the knot in June with country singer Kenny Chesney, 37, on St. John in the Virgin Islands, above. Perhaps the star of the *Bridget Jones* series is starting to identify with her screen alter ego: the pair filed for an annulment in September.

BEN & JENNIFER No, the natural mate for Ben Affleck, 33, apparently is not his longtime pal and *Good Will Hunting* co-creator Matt Damon. Instead, Affleck's romance with Jennifer Garner, 33, star of TV's *Alias,* culminated in a Caribbean wedding—and the news that she would give birth in the fall.

TOP TO BOTTOM: J. SCOTT APPLEWHITE—AP/WIDE WORLD (2); LEE MARRINER—AP/WIDE WORLD; TAMMIE ARROYO—AP/WIDE WORLD; DAVID LONGSTREATH—AP/WIDE WORLD; FITZROY BARRETT—GLOBE PHOTOS

ODD COUPLES

Let us not to the marriage of true minds admit impediments . . . especially in an America that seems to take perverse joy in its red state–blue state dichotomies. If Hillary Clinton and Newt Gingrich can appear together in harmony on the steps of the U.S. Capitol, what's to stop the rest of us from heeding political pundit Rodney King's famous 1992 plea: "Can we get along?"

BILL CLINTON & GEORGE H.W. BUSH If you think this is an unlikely liaison, consider the matchmaker: the two ex-Presidents teamed up at the request of President George W. Bush, who asked them to serve as co-heads of the U.S. effort to aid victims of the Indian Ocean tsunami of Dec. 26, 2004. The Oval Office veterans soon became fast friends, although reports that Barbara Bush calls Clinton "son" may be apocryphal. TIME's longtime White House watcher Hugh Sidey claims the affection between the two men is real, and he reports that the senior Bush, 81, professes to be amazed by the vitality of the younger man, now 59. In the wake of Hurricane Katrina, George W. Bush asked the two to recap their roles and lead fund-raising efforts to aid victims of the disaster.

NEWT GINGRICH & HILLARY CLINTON Joking that their joint appearance might be viewed as the sign of an impending doomsday, the junior Senator from New York State and the firebrand ex-Speaker who led the 1994 revolution that brought Republicans to power in the House came together outside the U.S. Capitol in May to promote legislation modernizing medical record keeping. Amid wide reports that Senator Clinton will make a run for the White House in 2008, political observers smelled a whiff of the strategy Bill Clinton used to defang Gingrich's 1994 victory: triangulation.

SANDRA BULLOCK & JESSE JAMES Maybe this one isn't so odd. Bullock, 41, is the rare Hollywood star who not only claims she doesn't care for the glitzy life but also seems to mean it: *Miss Congeniality* frequently forsakes the West Coast for her home in Austin, Texas, and she has stayed close to many of her old friends from her pre-*Speed,* pre-stardom days. In 2005 she cemented her dirt-under-the-nails image with her marriage to Jesse James, 35, the gearhead motorcycle mechanic who stars in Discovery Channel's *Monster Garage.* After they wed at a California ranch on July 16, Bullock dismissed tabloid descriptions of James as a "tattooed bad boy."

SocietyNotebook

Video Wars: The Next Front Line

Video games—long regarded as a time-wasting hobby for grumpy teens—have become a vital force in pop culture, helping turn U.S. living rooms into a digital, wireless, networked nerve center. Three companies—Nintendo, Sony and Microsoft—are battling to own the $25 billion global video-game market, and in the fall Microsoft upped the ante with its new Xbox 360 system, whose games—like *Call of Duty 2*, left—feature a high-definition, widescreen format and Dolby 5.1 surround sound. The 360 can also play songs off CDs (or an iPod) on its hard drive; its online service will allow players to chat free over long distances. Market leader Sony and lagging Nintendo will put their new systems on sale in 2006.

MICROSOFT

> **"**The data will, I am confident, reveal that Catholics are substantially underrepresented in investment banking … that white men are very substantially underrepresented in the National Basketball Association and that Jews are very substantially underrepresented in farming.**"**
>
> **—LAWRENCE SUMMERS,**
> *Harvard University president, in remarks at an academic conference in January, comparing those groups with women, who he noted are underrepresented in the fields of science and math. His comments drew intense fire for suggesting that innate gender differences, as well as social factors, might account for the academic gap*

AMY SANCETTA—AP/WIDE WORLD

Satellite Radio Turns Up the Volume

Like cable TV, satellite radio was once laughed at: pay $12.95 a month for radio? No way! Yet audience ratings are exploding for the two firms vying to rule the medium, XM Radio and Sirius. Free from content cops, satellite serves up crude fare you can't hear over the AM/FM dial. Small wonder trash-talking Howard Stern is joining DJ Dusty Street, left, at Sirius, which is wooing stars to catch up with market leader XM's superior technology.

Runaway Bride

Jennifer Wilbanks, a 32-year-old nurse from Duluth, Ga., was supposed to have been married to John Mason on April 30 in a swank affair at the Atlanta

Jennifer Carol Wilbanks
32 5'8" 123lbs
Brown hair / Brown eyes

MISSING

CASE SOLVED: COLD FEET
770-41...

Athletic Club featuring 600 guests, 14 bridesmaids and 14 groomsmen. But on April 26 Wilbanks went missing, and local authorities launched a massive manhunt to find her. Three days later Wilbanks was picked up in Albuquerque, N.M., after police traced a call she made from a pay phone to let Mason know she was alive. She told the police she had been kidnapped near her home and driven more than 1,000 miles to New Mexico, but they soon determined she was lying: suffering from cold feet, she had fled Georgia to escape the nuptials. It all seemed humorously reminiscent of the hit 1999 movie *Runaway Bride*—except to furious Duluth authorities, who had expended $43,000 searching for her. On June 2 Wilbanks pleaded no contest to a felony charge of providing false information to police; in a plea bargain, she was sentenced to two years' probation and 120 hours of community service.

RIC FELD—AP/WIDE WORLD

Police Blotter

The wheels of justice grind slowly: it was back in 2001 that a series of corporate scandals and bankruptcies first began tarnishing the image of Big Business in the U.S. In 2005 three former top executives were found guilty or sentenced, and one was acquitted, in cases of big-time corporate crime.

BERNIE EBBERS The former CEO of telecom industry giant WorldCom was found guilty of fraud and conspiracy in March. His sentence: 25 years in a federal prison.

JOHN RIGAS The founder of cable company Adelphia, charged with his sons and other execs of looting the firm into bankruptcy, was found guilty in 2004. He was sentenced to 15 years in prison in 2005.

RICHARD SCRUSHY The former CEO of health-care firm HealthSouth, charged with reporting false earnings, was acquitted on June 28 of 36 counts of fraud and conspiracy.

DENNIS KOZLOWSKI After a 2004 mistrial, the high-living former boss of conglomerate Tyco was found guilty of misappro–priation of corporate funds in June; the case is under appeal.

The Jerry Springer of Stock Pickers

Jim Cramer's knack for quick stock analysis made him a fortune on Wall Street in the '90s; now it's helping him revive ratings at financial cable station CNBC. On *Mad Money with Jim Cramer,* the blustery investment whiz bounces around the set howling stock-market strategy, aided by a range of silly sound effects. Result: CNBC's viewership is sky-rocketing. Buy!

FROM TOP: LOUIS LANZANO—AP/WIDE WORLD (2); BUTCH DILL—AP/WIDE WORLD; GREGORY BULL—AP/WIDE WORLD

Drawing Board

..DO YOU HAVE A RESERVATION?

Le Gas

caglecartoons.com

TAB—THE CALGARY SUN/CAGLE CARTOONS

Martha's Trek: From the Big House to Your House

Americans love a survivor, as a certain successful TV show amply demonstrates. So broadcast executives were hoping that viewers would take to two new fall offerings from homemaking doyen Martha Stewart, who on March 4 was released from a federal prison in West Virginia, where she had served a five-month term after being found guilty of lying to federal agents investigating a securities case. (Her first home meal: risotto.)

The resilient Stewart, whose business empire took a hit during her legal trials, returned from the prison toting a poncho knit for her by a fellow prisoner, right, and sporting an ankle bracelet to help enforce her house arrest. In September she launched her new TV series, teaming up with Donald Trump and reality-TV guru Mark Burnett on a version of Trump's ongoing NBC hit *The Apprentice,* even while firing up the burners for a syndicated daily domestic-arts show, *Martha.*

MARY ALTAFFER—AP/WIDE WORLD

Sport

NICOLAS ASFOURI—AFP—GETTY IMAGES

TIMELESS

Along with baseball, golf is one of the few sports not subject
to the tyranny of the clock: there's no 24-second rule to hurry
players along as they size up a critical putt. And golfers, alone
among athletes of major sports, beat the clock in an even more
satisfying way: they can keep playing well into their senior
years, burnishing legends and delighting fans for decades.
When the man widely considered the game's greatest player,
Jack Nicklaus, announced that the 2005 British Open would
be his last major tournament, it marked the 37th time that
Nicklaus, 65, had contended for the claret jug that goes to
the event's winner. Nicklaus missed the cut in the tournament—
held, fittingly, at the cradle of the game, the Old Course at St.
Andrews in Scotland—but he finished his last round in classic
style. After basking in a thunderous round of applause as he
paused on the historic Swilcan bridge that leads to the
venerable course's 18th hole, he strode to the green,
drew a bead on the cup and rolled in a birdie putt.

Danica Patrick

SUCCESSFULLY EXECUTING A TRICKY MANEUVER THAT Dale Earnhardt never quite mastered—the hair flip—Danica Patrick became the biggest story in American auto racing in 2005. The one accessory the rookie Indy Racing League driver most desired, a checkered flag, eluded her, but she made good progress toward a larger goal: focusing attention on her talents rather than her gender. At the Indianapolis 500, Patrick, 23, became the first woman to hold a lead in the race. Winner Dan Wheldon passed her with six laps to go, and she ended up placing fourth. But TV ratings soared for Patrick's IRL open-wheel racing circuit, which has struggled to win fans even as the stock-car drivers of NASCAR continue to enjoy roaring success.

After losing the 500, Patrick earned the pole position for the July 3 IRL race in Kansas City, Kans., but faded and finished ninth. Two weeks later she led the pack for nine laps at the Firestone Indy 200 in Nashville, Tenn., but couldn't hang on to the lead. No matter: the 30,000-seat Nashville Speedway had failed to sell out in 2004, yet thanks to "Danica Mania," it was packed to capacity in 2005. Patrick ended the 2005 season with six top-10 finishes on the IRL circuit and was crowned its Rookie of the Year.

At 5 ft. 2 in. and 100 lbs., the Wisconsin-born Patrick faces charges that her light weight gives her an unfair advantage on the track; she points out that the heaviest car in the race won the Indy 500 in 2004. Dilatory off the track, Patrick told TIME she struggles with procrastination, yet she went on to admit, "I hate slow drivers. I hate left-lane drivers—if you're going to drive slow, just drive on the side. I have road rage every day. Every day." ■

JONATHAN FERREY—GETTY IMAGES

Lance Armstrong

THE MONTHS AFTER THE GREAT CYCLIST WON HIS SEV-enth Tour de France in July may have reminded Lance Armstrong of the up-and-down terrain he thought he had left behind in the Pyrenees. On Aug. 20, he visited the Crawford, Texas, ranch of President George W. Bush, where the world's toughest biker and the leader of the free world shared a 17-mile outing. The cancer survivor, 34, lobbied Bush to funnel more money into cancer research and learned that Bush was reappointing him to a presidential advisory panel that oversees the effort—despite the fact that Armstrong, who may be eyeing a future in politics, has been a critic of the war in Iraq and met with another ad-mirer, Senator John Kerry, during the Tour de France.

Yet all this must have seemed like background noise when new allegations—actually new stories about old alle-gations—were published on Aug. 23 by the French sports daily *L'Equipe*, accusing Armstrong of testing positive for the performance-enhancing drug EPO in the 1999 Tour. The outraged athlete called the story a "witch hunt." He was vindicated weeks later, when the International Cycling Union, the sport's governing body, issued a statement say-ing it had seen no evidence of Armstrong's having used such substances and criticizing both *L'Equipe* and French cycling authorities for making irresponsible accusations.

Armstrong finally seemed to shift into a more relaxed gear with the Sept. 5 announcement that he and his girl-friend, rock musician Sheryl Crow, 43, had decided to mar-ry. But the charges of *L'Equipe* may have put a burr under the saddle of the man who declared on winning his seventh Tour that he felt sorry for the sport's "cynics." Although he had announced his retirement in July with the words "I'm finished," Armstrong revealed in September that he was going to enter winter training with his old team and began hinting that he might just keep pedaling after all. ∎

Michelle Wie

GOLF'S NEWEST STAR FOUND HERSELF IN SOME TOUGH SPOTS in 2005: she faced a tricky lie in the rough on the 14th hole of the last round of the LPGA Championship; she had to master parallel parking to get her driver's permit; and the final exams of her sophomore year in high school were, like, totally harsh. Yes, Michelle Wie is now all of 16, and the 6-ft. Hawaii native, whose drives sail 300 yds., has set herself a goal worthy of a teen: she wants to compete against the sport's top pros—and that means not only Annika Sorenstam and Paula Creamer of the LPGA but also the PGA's Tiger, Woods, Phil Mickelson and Ernie Els.

Will she get there? The jury is still out. Wie kicked off the year at a men's PGA event, the Sony Open in Hawaii, where in 2004 she had missed the cut by only a stroke; this year she putted poorly and missed the cut by seven strokes. In July she became the first woman to qualify for a men's USGA championship when she reached the quarterfinals of the Amateur Public Links tourney.

In women's play, Wie finished second to Sorenstam at the LPGA Championship in Maryland early in June, although, as an amateur, she couldn't enjoy the $164,385 second-place purse. Two weeks later she shared the lead going into the last round of the U.S. Women's Open in Minnesota, then imploded, shooting 82. By the fall of 2005, Wie had passed up more than $600,000 in LPGA prize money by refusing to turn pro. So no one was too surprised when the young star announced on Oct. 5 that she would compete as a professional on the women's tour and continue to play in men's events when possible.

Will Michelle face Tiger for a PGA title someday? If she does, she already has a nickname, courtesy of veteran pro Tom Lehman. With a nod to Els, known as "the Big Easy," Lehman calls his young pal "the Big Wiesy." ∎

Manu Ginobili

H E SLITHERS, HE SWERVES, HE SQUIRMS! HE FAKES left, moves right! He shoots, he scores! And yes, when he's chasing a loose ball, Manu Ginobili has even been known to crawl on his belly like a reptile. Manu, as all roundball fans call him, is the best thing to happen to the NBA since Michael Jordan first pulled on a Bulls jersey. The Argentine, 28, led the San Antonio Spurs to the championship in 2005, just as he led his nation's team to victory over the U.S. in the semifinals of the 2004 Olympics, on the way to the gold medal. With his manic, unpredictable style, the shooting guard brings a jolting spark of electricity to a professional game that badly needs both new energy and new stars. Deadly from the three-point zone, the 6-ft. 6-in. star is even more thrilling when he squeezes into the tiniest of spaces between two foes, then finds an opening and uncoils to throw down a huge dunk. With his good looks, long hair and refreshing accessibility (he often answers e-mails from fans personally on the website he maintains), Manu is a magnet for female fans; as an Argentine who is teaching Americans new tricks in a game that was born in the U.S.A., he is the poster boy for a sport that is surging in popularity around the world. ∎

WOODS: The new two-time champ smooches the Claret Jug after his victory at St. Andrew's

JAMIE SQUIRE—GETTY IMAGES

LOOK WHO'S BACK ON TOP

A resurgent Tiger Woods wins his ninth and 10th major tournaments, while Phil Mickelson, the longtime gallery favorite, snags his second

WHAT A DIFFERENCE A YEAR MAKES. AS THE 2004 PGA season ended, Vijay Singh (of the smooth swing) had brought high-flying Tiger Woods, the game's longtime No. 1 player, down to earth. While Woods, 30, had spent the year retooling his swing for the second time in his pro career, Singh, 42, had gone on a tear: he won an incredible nine PGA tournaments, pocketed a record-setting $10.9 million in earnings and snatched Woods' crown as No. 1. Phil Mickelson, 34, was also in on the chase: he won his first major tournament in 2004, the Masters, and by season's end the gregarious "Lefty" was No. 4 in the world rankings. But what made the three-way matchup so spicy was that the players are not exactly three amigos.

Call it golf's little soap opera. Mickelson—whose perpetual boyish cheer in the world's most frustrating sport irks the intense Woods and Singh—had annoyed Woods by criticizing his Nike woods in 2003. As for Singh, the big Fijian has never pretended to be a nice guy: he memorably dissed Woods' pal Annika Sorenstam in 2003, saying the LPGA great didn't "belong out here" when she played in the PGA Colonial Tournament. Singh's caddie once wore a ballcap with the inscription TIGER WHO? So as Woods, Singh and Mickelson teed up at the year's first major event, the Masters, the stage was set for a season-long tussle at the top.

By year's end, the golf gods had spoken: comeback kid Tiger had won two majors; ever chipper Phil had won one; and, well, the fat lady had sung for Vijay, winless in the 2005 majors. (Spare your tears, Singh fans: by December, he had won four tournaments and earned $8 million.)

Woods started strong in April, conjuring up one of his greatest days during Sunday's long session at the Masters. After rain halted play during Saturday's third round, Tiger was trailing Chris DiMarco by four strokes. Early Sunday morning, when play resumed, Woods charged, making up the deficit to draw even with DiMarco in the first two holes.

FRED VUICH—SPORTS ILLUSTRATED

MICKELSON: "Lefty" blasts out of a bunker on his way to the PGA title

CAMPBELL **When two-time U.S. Open champ Retief Goosen fell apart after leading through three rounds, the Kiwi took the lead and held it, fending off a strong charge by Woods**

ROBERT BECK—SPORTS ILLUSTRATED

He went on to notch an incredible seven birdies in a row, coming out of the third round with a three-shot lead. Moving immediately into fourth-round play, Tiger began to wobble, hitting a few poor shots, but thrilled the gallery with a classic 25-ft. chip shot on the 16th hole that hung forever on the lip of the cup, then dropped in for a birdie.

Yet now Tiger's tank seemed out of gas: with victory in sight, he bogeyed the last two holes, and DiMarco drew even. But Tiger slammed the door on the first playoff hole, sinking a 15-ft. birdie putt to win his fourth Masters in nine attempts—a statistic that underlines his recent dominance of the game. The victory also earned back his ranking as the game's No. 1 player, ousting Singh—who vented his ire at Mickelson, accusing him of ruining Augusta National's greens with his long spikes, keeping their catfight alive.

Woods kept charging at June's U.S. Open at Pinehurst, N.C. In the final round, Tiger chased the leader, New Zealand's Mike Campbell, in memorable fashion: eight shots behind heading into the third hole, he was only two shots behind by the 12th. But he again faltered at the end, bogeying 16 and 17, and Campbell was victorious.

There was no faltering for Woods at the next major, the British Open in July at St. Andrews in Scotland: he was a model of consistency, winning by five strokes to become only the second player ever to win all four majors at least twice. The other: his hero, Jack Nicklaus. Tiger's victory was his 10th in a major, putting him that much closer to his longtime goal, surpassing Nicklaus' total of 18 major wins.

At the PGA Championship in August, it was Mickelson's turn. He owned the Baltusrol course in New Jersey, leading all four rounds, then allowing two competitors to get close at the finish just to keep things interesting and, finally, rolling in a birdie putt on the 72nd hole to win his second major tournament, delighting his army of fans.

By December, Tiger was in command at No. 1, with six PGA wins (including the stroke-play Buick Invitational) and $10.6 million in prize money; Vijay was No. 2; Phil was No. 3. What's next, golf lovers? Will Tiger catch Jack? Will Vijay catch Tiger? Will Lefty and Vijay kiss and make up? Will Singh's caddie figure out Tiger's last name? Stay tuned for the 2006 edition of *As the Tee Turns.* ∎

ANNIKA—AND EVERYBODY ELSE

ANDY LYONS—GETTY IMAGES

SORENSTAM **The Swede "is toying with us," said veteran pro Laura Davies**

Annika Sorenstam and Tiger Woods are tops in their leagues, but even Tiger couldn't match the impetus with which his good friend entered the 2005 LPGA season. After winning her last two 2004 events, Sorenstam won the first two tournaments of 2005, then dominated the year's first major tourney, the Nabisco Championship at Mission Hills in Rancho Mirage, Calif., cruising to an eight-stroke win. The string of five successive victories tied a record set by Nancy Lopez in 1978 and had fans of the women's game buzzing about a potential Grand Slam.

The buzz grew to a roar in June, when Sorenstam, 34, took the slam's second leg, the LPGA Championship at Maryland's Bulle Rock course, winning by three strokes. It was her ninth major championship, and she celebrated by sending Woods a friendly two-digit text message noting their new stand-off in major titles: "9-9."

But the Soren-slam was not to be. The Swede struggled from the get-go at the U.S. Women's Open at Cherry Hills outside Denver and tied for 23rd place. Birdie Kim, 23, took the title with a fine 30-yd. chip shot from the bunker on the 72nd hole that rolled in for a ... yes, birdie. Another Seoul sister, previously unsung journeywoman Jeong Jang, won the Women's British Open at Scotland's Royal Birkdale course on July 31; Annika tied for fifth. Current standings: Tiger, 10; Annika, 9. But wait until next year.

BIRDIE KIM: **She changed her name from Ju Yun Kim to stand out among a crowded field of LPGA Kims**

CHRIS CARLSON—AP/WIDE WORLD

BEST IN SHOW, 2005

A fence-climbing driver, a shorthaired pointer, an airborne Venus and a solo sailor lead the parade of the year's sporting champs

AFLEET ALEX The year's best horse won the last two legs of the Triple Crown—even coming back from a far-turn stumble to take the Preakness Stakes, shown here. But Afleet Alex lost the first leg, the Kentucky Derby, by one length to 50-to-1 long-shot Giacomo

JOE CAVARETTA—AP/WIDE WORLD

SAN ANTONIO SPURS Low-key Tim Duncan, above, and wild man Manu Ginobili led their team to the NBA title

ELLEN MACARTHUR The gritty Brit, 30, set a new, solo nonstop round-the-world sailing record of 71 days, 14 hr., 18 min. Below, she sails her 75-ft. trimaran *B&Q Castorama* into Falmouth Harbor on Feb. 8

FRANKA BRUNS—AP/WIDE WORLD

VENUS WILLIAMS Back from a long slump, Serena's big sister lifts off after beating defending champ Maria Sharapova in the semifinals at Wimbledon. Williams went on to edge out Lindsay Davenport in a classic final match

NEW ENGLAND PATRIOTS Wow! Bill Belichick's resilient Pats became the NFL's first dynasty of the new century, beating Philly's Eagles 24-21 to win three of the past four Super Bowls

CARLEE The German shorthaired pointer, a.k.a. Ch. Kan-Point's VJK Autumn Roses, was named Best in Show at the annual Westminster Kennel Club meet. She's ready for her close-up

DOUG PENSINGER—GETTY IMAGES

TONY STEWART The popular NASCAR driver—who toasts each win with a fence-climbing routine—had already scrambled aloft five times by Labor Day, holding off Jimmie Johnson and Greg Biffle as the circuit's leader

Sport Notebook

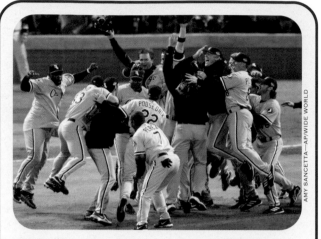

AMY SANCETTA—AP/WIDE WORLD

White Sox Win Series, Reverse the Curse

Baseball fans may have thought they had seen it all when the long-suffering Boston Red Sox managed to win a World Series in 2004, after a drought of 86 years. But 2005 brought another longtime band of cellar dwellers to the top of baseball's heap, as an engaging team of Chicago White Sox players finally erased the haunting memories of the Series-throwing "Black Sox" team of 1919. Led by their charming, garrulous manager, former White Sox shortstop Ozzie Guillen, the Pale Hose first tromped the Los Angeles Angels in the League Championship Series, then swept the Houston Astros in the World Series, making Windy City rivals the Chicago Cubs the last of the sport's perennial losers.

A Season in the Slow Lane for No. 8

What's ailing Junior? After the death of NASCAR great Dale Earnhardt in 2001, fans embraced his son and namesake, making him the circuit's most popular driver. Dale Jr. had a strong year in 2004, but scenes like the one above—No. 8 pumping his arms aloft, enjoying a Budweiser shower after winning the USG Sheetrock 400 race at Chicagoland Speedway on July 10—were scarce in 2005. At season's end, the Sheetrock was his only victory, and No. 8 finished in 19th place among drivers, failing to make the cut to join the chase for the Nextel Cup. Junior's vow: wait until next year, when he will reunite with the crew chief with whom he parted ways in 2004, cousin Tony Eury Jr.

A New Generation of Conquistadors Takes to the Court

Tennis, long in need of fresh faces, is finally serving up some aces. Maria Sharapova, 18, who won at Wimbledon in 2004, went winless in the majors this year, but the 6-ft. 2-in. Russian beauty claims she's still growing, and so are her skills. On the men's side, fans loved the swashbuckling Spaniard Rafael Nadal, 19, who boasted powerful ground strokes and hunky looks—not to mention his cool pirate pants and 2005 French Open trophy. And familiarity is finally breeding affection for Roger Federer, right, already an old-timer at age 24. The steady Swiss proved he is one of the game's all-time greats, winning his third Wimbledon and second U.S. Open titles.

FROM LEFT: FRANCOIS MORI—AP/WIDE WORLD (2); ANJA NIEDRINGHAUS—AP/WIDE WORLD

Robots, Start Your Camels

Yes, it sounds like a fake news story from the *Onion:* in the United Arab Emirates, where camel racing is Big Business, track directors commissioned the creation of remote-controlled robot jockeys to ride the hump-backed beasts. In fact, the robots are a human-rights success story: they will replace thousands of boys, many of them under age 12, who have been dragooned into virtual slavery and kept underfed in order to reduce the camels' burden.

> **"** Everybody out there who calls us spoiled because we play 'a game'—they can kiss my a__ … We don't want you in the rink, we don't want you in the stadium, we don't want you to watch hockey. **"**

—JEREMY ROENICK,
Philadelphia Flyers center, in response to fans who criticized NHL players for their role in the cancellation of the 2004 season

The Last Count?
After losing decisively to unheralded Irish journeyman Kevin McBride on June 11, former heavyweight champ Mike Tyson, 40, vowed to hang up his gloves. "My heart isn't into this anymore. I don't want to disrespect the sport I love," said Iron Mike.

NEIL LEIFER—SPORTS ILLUSTRATED

Drawing Board

MIKE SMITH—LAS VEGAS SUN/KING FEATURES SYNDICATE

FINALLY, NASA FIGURED OUT A WAY TO MAKE THE SHUTTLE RELIABLE.

JANE MINGAY—AP/WIDE WORLD

London Is Lord of the Rings
London sent PM Tony Blair, soccer player David Beckham and runner Sebastian Coe to the decisive meeting in Singapore. New York City sent Senator Hillary Clinton and Mayor Michael Bloomberg. Bookmakers made Paris the favorite. But in July, after two years of wooing, the International Olympic Committee chose London as the site of the 2012 Summer Games.

Bound for Baseball's Hall of Shame?

Say it ain't so, Rafael Palmeiro! In March, when six current and former major league ballplayers appeared before the House Government Reform Committee, which was investigating charges of steroid abuse in baseball, the Baltimore Orioles great jabbed a finger at Congressmen and said, "I have never used steroids. Period." His testimony was convincing, in contrast to that of former St. Louis Cardinals slugger Mark McGwire. Big Mac, who looked far more svelte than in his bulked-up playing days, sheltered himself behind a gutless statement that had been carefully vetted by his lawyers.

Five months later, the shoe dropped: on Aug. 2, Palmeiro, 40, was suspended from play for 10 days. He was the seventh player to fail a drug test under the major leagues' new, tougher antisteroids policy. Once a sure bet for the Hall of Fame, Palmeiro may have trouble getting to Cooperstown.

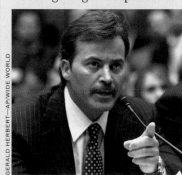

GERALD HERBERT—AP/WIDE WORLD

Science

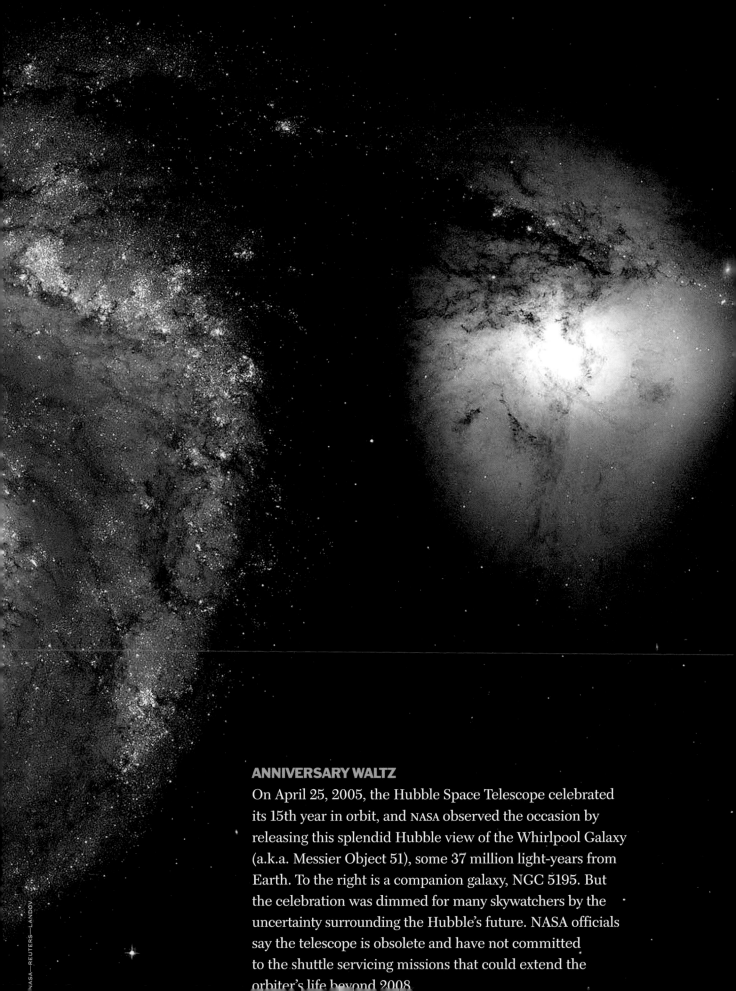

NASA—REUTERS—LANDOV

ANNIVERSARY WALTZ

On April 25, 2005, the Hubble Space Telescope celebrated
its 15th year in orbit, and NASA observed the occasion by
releasing this splendid Hubble view of the Whirlpool Galaxy
(a.k.a. Messier Object 51), some 37 million light-years from
Earth. To the right is a companion galaxy, NGC 5195. But
the celebration was dimmed for many skywatchers by the
uncertainty surrounding the Hubble's future. NASA officials
say the telescope is obsolete and have not committed
to the shuttle servicing missions that could extend the
orbiter's life beyond 2008.

Snuppy

MEET THE WORLD'S FIRST CLONED DOG, SNUPPY (FOR Seoul National University puppy), below. The Aug. 3 news of the Afghan pup's birth seemed a crowning moment for Woo Suk Hwang, for it was the second of two achievements claimed by the veterinary scientist in 2005. Hwang first made headlines around the world—and was celebrated as a hero in South Korea—in May, when his team announced in a paper in the respected journal *Science* that they had become the first to use cloning techniques to create stem cells from human patients suffering from conditions such as diabetes and spinal-cord injury. Tissue derived from those cells could, in theory, be implanted in the pancreas or spine with little chance that the body would reject it; if successful, the same approach could be applied to other parts of the body.

But Hwang's year ended in disgrace; it now seems possible that his name will be remembered more in sorrow than honor. He resigned from his post at a high-profile new stem-cell research center in November, after it was revealed that he had lied about the source of some of the human eggs used in his medical research. In December a U.S. scientist who had co-signed the *Science* paper announcing the stem-cell breakthrough withdrew his name from it, and several investigations are now underway to determine if the research was falsified. ∎

Ivory-Billed Woodpecker

SORRY, FOLKS: WE CAN'T SHOW YOU THE face of a living ivory-billed woodpecker, and neither can the researchers who say they have located the bird—previously last seen in the wild in 1944—alive and pecking in the swamps of eastern Arkansas. For now, the stuffed specimen here will have to do. The big woodpecker had been feared extinct, and the news that a breeding pair might be alive sent chills down the spines of birding enthusiasts and scientists around the world when it was announced in a *Science* magazine article on April 28 by a team from the Ornithology Laboratory at Cornell University. Some birders had taken to calling the ivory-bill the "Grail bird": a sighting of it was long their Holy Grail.

The bird was first spotted in February 2004 by kayaker Gene Sparling of Hot Springs, Ark., who later led two ornithologists to the site, deep in the Big Woods of Arkansas at the Cache River National Wildlife Refuge; they also saw the bird. In all, 15 sightings were made in 2004 and '05, seven of which were featured in the *Science* article; a fuzzy four-second video seemed to show the bird in flight. Some scholars questioned the original report, but they were convinced when they heard a recording that clearly captured the ivory-bill's unique, two-beat peck.

Why all the fuss? To begin with, the bird is a beauty—standing 18 to 20 in. high, it sports brilliant plumage, a noble wingspan and a snazzy red crest. More important, the survival of the bird would validate the efforts of a host of conservation agencies, birders and scientists who have labored for decades to conserve America's natural heritage. ■

JOHN CANCALOSI—PETER ARNOLD INC.

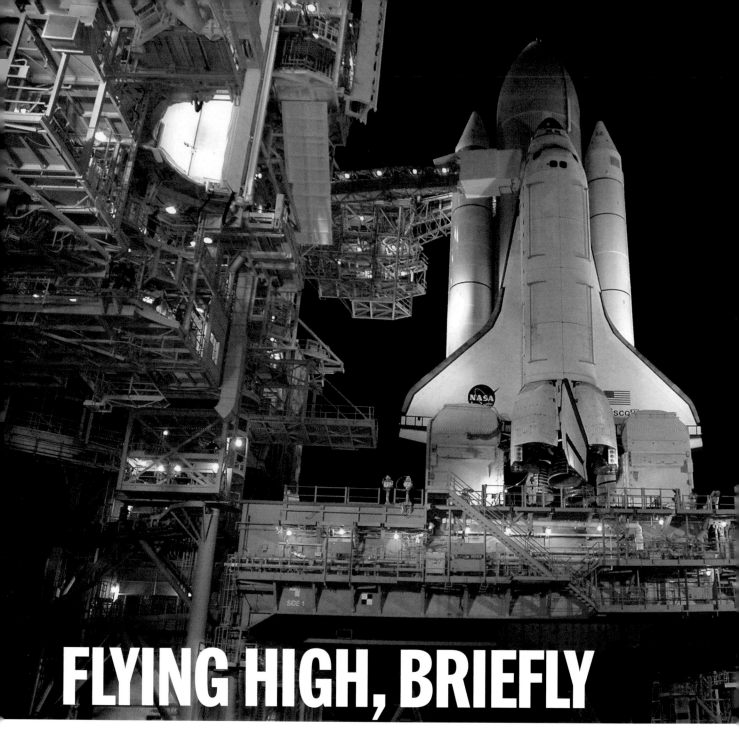

FLYING HIGH, BRIEFLY

Discovery lifts off into space and America's embattled shuttle program
flies again, but a glitch-filled flight puts the future, well, up in the air

AT 10:39 A.M. E.T. ON JULY 26, AMERICANS LISTENED TO
the words they had been longing to hear for more
than two years: "Liftoff of space shuttle *Discovery*,"
intoned George Diller, voice of NASA Mission Control,
"beginning America's new journey to the moon, Mars and
beyond." If the pronouncement sounded a bit grand, it was
hard to begrudge the space agency a moment of swagger;
NASA had been licking its wounds since the 2003 *Columbia* disaster, when a piece of insulating foam on a fuel tank
broke free on launch and damaged the tiles that protect the
shuttle from temperatures hot enough to melt steel as it
re-enters Earth's atmosphere. *Columbia* had broken into
pieces on re-entry, and all seven crew members had died.

In the wake of the tragedy, NASA's three shuttles were
grounded while NASA engineers worked feverishly to prevent a recurrence of the problem, spending $1 billion to re-
design the foam insulation and the exterior fuel tank it
protects. The space agency declared it was working just as
hard to create a new culture that emphasized astronaut
safety, although some critics were skeptical of that claim.

Discovery's launch date was set for July 13, but whether
as a result of new safety protocols or just plain jitters, the
long-awaited liftoff was delayed for almost two weeks by
what previously would have been regarded as a minor
glitch: a faulty fuel sensor in *Discovery's* external tank. Another sign of NASA's new vigilance was the array of 107

CLOCKWISE FROM TOP LEFT: NASA VIA GETTY IMAGES (2); NASA

POISED At left, *Discovery* waits on the launch pad on the night before blast-off, July 25

PERCH At top, astronaut Steve Robinson, on a repair mission, takes a ride into space on *Discovery's* robot arm on Aug. 3

CLOSE-UP The picture at left above, taken from the International Space Station, was used by NASA mission commanders to assess damage to protective tiles

ASTRONAUTS Above right, the crew. From left, Charlie Camarda, Andy Thomas, Soichi Noguchi, Wendy Lawrence, Steve Robinson, mission commander Eileen Collins, James Kelly

liver much needed supplies to the International Space Station. Concerned NASA officials ordered the craft to make a complete 360° belly-flop as it approached the orbiter, so station cameras could search for damage on its underside.

The pictures, augmented by photos taken from the shuttle's 50-ft. arm, detected at least 25 dings in *Discovery's* insulating tiles. The most worrisome: a 1.5-in. divot near the nose, where temperatures can reach 3000°F. In addition, the photos showed that two pieces of "gap filler"—thin fabric, stiffened with a ceramic material, that plugs crevices between the shuttle's heat-resistant tiles—were protruding from *Discovery's* underside. The next day, NASA declared that it was once again grounding the entire shuttle fleet indefinitely, while embarrassed engineers explained that the safety upgrades they had designed were meant to minimize falling pieces of foam, rather than eliminate them entirely, a goal considered impossible to achieve.

All of which left a large question: how to ensure *Discovery's* safe return. To accomplish that, astronaut Steve Robinson performed an unprecedented shuttle repair mission while in orbit. During a 56-min. spacewalk, Robinson checked out the damaged tiles on the shuttle's underside and plucked out the loose pieces of gap filler. Although equipped with a high-tech tool kit, Robinson ended up using his gloved hand to grab the material. NASA's mission controllers considered a second spacewalk to repair other damaged areas but decided the damage was so minor that attempting to repair it was riskier than doing nothing.

Even so, tension ran high as *Discovery* turned toward home. The initial plan called for a landing at the Florida space center. It was delayed for one day by bad weather, then canceled entirely, and the shuttle was directed to its secondary landing site at Edwards Air Force Base in California. Finally, at 5:11 a.m. on Aug. 9, *Discovery* touched down safely in the desert—and early-rising Americans exhaled as one, in a collective sigh of relief. Afterward, deputy shuttle program manager Wayne Hale would admit that "my heart has been in my throat all morning." Mission commander Eileen Collins struck a more positive note, saying modestly, "We're happy to be back."

Yes, the space agency was flying again—for all of 14 days. Now the question is not the fate of *Discovery* but that of NASA's entire manned space program. After two years and $1 billion spent on safety upgrades designed to prevent just such a setback, how could things go so wrong again? Can a shuttle program that has already claimed the lives of 14 astronauts ever be safe? And what about the International Space Station? Is it worth the effort and money that the U.S. will have to pour into supplying it to keep it aloft?

Discovery, Endeavour, and *Atlantis* are now grounded for the short run, and the shuttle program is scheduled to end no later than 2010. But the vehicle that will replace the shuttles has yet to be built—or even fully designed. In the meantime, spacecraft that are decades old will have to continue hauling people and hardware into orbit, if plans for the space station and "America's new journey to the moon, Mars and beyond" are to move forward. For now, the shuttles and NASA aren't going anywhere until the space agency's engineers take a much shorter journey—back to the drawing board. ∎

high-resolution cameras, mounted both on the ground and aboard aircraft circling above, all looking for any sign of the kind of damage that brought down *Columbia.*

So it was with some disappointment and more concern that NASA acknowledged, after poring over liftoff images gathered by these cameras, that several pieces of insulation had broken off from the launch booster once again. In all, four pieces of insulating foam—the largest the size of a skateboard—had spun off the ship's external fuel tank during liftoff. Although this was exactly the kind of debris that had damaged *Columbia's* wing and doomed the ship, only one small piece appeared to have struck *Discovery* this time, glancing off a wing with so little force it didn't register on impact sensors. "The cameras worked well," said NASA chief Michael Griffin. "The foam did not."

Once aloft, the shuttle's first item of business was to de-

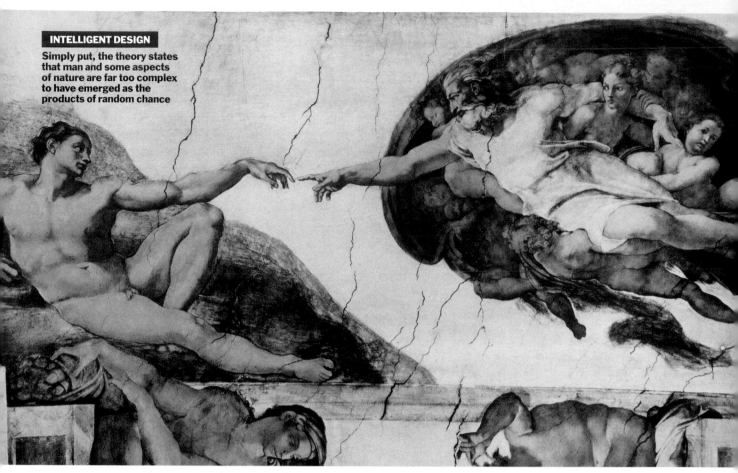

INTELLIGENT DESIGN
Simply put, the theory states that man and some aspects of nature are far too complex to have emerged as the products of random chance

AT WAR OVER EVOLUTION

President Bush joins the fray as controversial questions plague schools: Is "intelligent design" a real science—and should it be taught in class?

BETTMANN CORBIS

PRESIDENT GEORGE W. BUSH TURNED UP THE HEAT ON a pot that was already close to boiling over in August when he weighed in on the controversy over whether the teaching of evolution in school science classes should be accompanied by lessons in "intelligent design" —the proposition that some aspects of living things are best explained by an intelligent cause or agent, as opposed to the process of natural selection first advanced by Charles Darwin in the 19th century. In a question-and-answer session with Texas newspaper reporters, Bush said, "Both sides ought to be properly taught … so people can understand what the debate is about." Appearing to choose his words carefully, he continued, "I think that part of education is to expose people to different schools of thought."

On its surface, the President's position seemed fair-minded: What could possibly be wrong with presenting more than one point of view on a topic that divides so many Americans? But to biologists, it smacked of faith-based science and was especially suspect for coming at a time when U.S. science is perceived as being under fresh assault politically and competitively. In 2005, developments ranging from flaws in the space program to South Korea's rapid advances in the field of cloning were cited as examples that the U.S. is losing its edge in science.

For many Americans, however, the President may not have gone far enough. In a Harris poll conducted in June, 55% of 1,000 adults surveyed said children should be taught creationism and intelligent design along with evolution in public schools. The same poll found that 54% did not believe humans had developed from an earlier species—up from 45% with that view in 1994—although other polls have not detected this rise.

For these people there can be no reconciling of faith with Darwinism. It's little wonder, then, that almost one-third of the 1,050 teachers who responded to a National Science Teachers Association online survey in March said they had felt pressured by parents and students to include lessons on intelligent design, creationism or other nonscientific alternatives to evolution in their science classes; 30% of the teachers noted that they also had

COAST-TO-COAST CHALLENGES

Across the U.S., states and localities have considered changing the way biological evolution is taught. Some call for critical analysis of the theory; others seek equal time for intelligent design and creationism

Antievolution proposals considered since 2001 by:

▢	**State board of education**
▨	**State legislature**
▪	**Both**
●	**Local schools or panels** (2005 only)

EVOLUTION

Almost 150 years after it was proposed by Charles Darwin in *The Origin of Species* (1859), the theory still divides Americans

STAPLETON COLLECTION—CORBIS

teaching evolution. When such laws were struck down by a Supreme Court decision in 1968, some states instead required that "creation science" be taught alongside evolution. Supreme Court rulings in 1982 and 1987 put an end to that. Offering creationism in public schools, even as a side dish to evolution, the high court held, violated the First Amendment's separation of church and state.

But some anti-Darwinists seized upon Justice Antonin Scalia's dissenting opinion in the 1987 case. Christian Fundamentalists, he wrote, "are quite entitled, as a secular matter, to have whatever scientific evidence there may be against evolution presented in their schools." That line of argument—an emphasis on weaknesses and gaps in evolution—is at the heart of the intelligent-design movement, which has as its motto "Teach the controversy."

Darwin doubters used to focus on local schools; now they have a relatively new target, statewide curriculum standards for science. "Savvy creationists are focusing their efforts on this relatively new arena," says Glenn Branch of the National Center for Science Education. "The decision-making bodies involved in approving state science standards tend to be small, not particularly knowledgeable and, above all, elected, so it's a good opportunity for political pressure to be applied."

The momentum is not entirely on the side of Darwin doubters, however. In a blistering decision in a closely watched case in Delaware, Federal Judge John E. Jones ruled on Dec. 20 that the Dover Area School Board improperly introduced religion into the classroom when it required science teachers to read a brief statement in biology classes explaining that evolution is "just a theory." Judge Jones rejected any suggestion that evolution is somehow at odds with religion and described the arguments of school board members who claimed intelligent design is a science as "breathtaking inanity."

More battles are looming over the teaching of evolution in the many states that are preparing new standards-based tests in science. By raising the profile of intelligent design, President Bush not only emboldened those who differ with Darwin, but he also furthered the current goal of that movement: he taught all of us the controversy. ∎

been pressured to omit evolution from their curriculum.

Darwin's theory has been a hard sell to Americans ever since it was unveiled in *The Origin of Species*. The intelligent-design movement is just the latest and most sophisticated attempt to discredit the theory, which many Americans believe leaves insufficient room for the influence of God. In one early effort to thwart Darwin, Tennessee famously banned the teaching of evolution and convicted schoolteacher John Scopes of violating that ban in the "monkey trial" of 1925. At the time, two other states—Florida and Oklahoma—had laws that interfered with

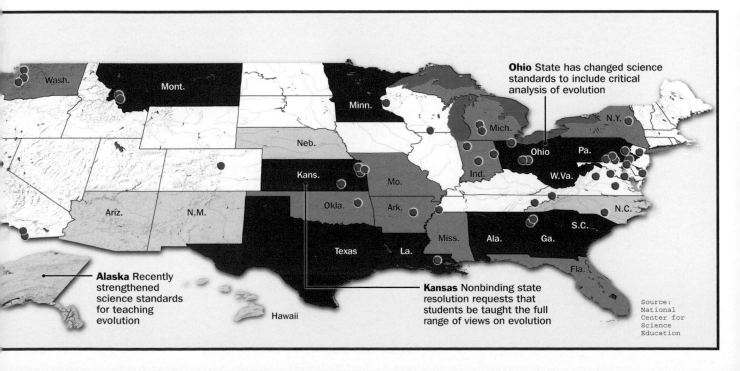

Ohio State has changed science standards to include critical analysis of evolution

Alaska Recently strengthened science standards for teaching evolution

Kansas Nonbinding state resolution requests that students be taught the full range of views on evolution

Source: National Center for Science Education

ScienceNotebook

Twilight Time on the Red Planet

This is what sunset looks like on Mars—or, to be precise, what it looked like on Saturday, June 11, 2005, from within the planet's Gusev Crater. The picture was taken by NASA's Spirit exploration vehicle, still operating long after it was expected to shut down, as was its counterpart Sojourner. The sun, millions of miles further away from the Red Planet than it is from ours, is about two-thirds the size it appears to be from Earth. The thin Martian atmosphere makes spaces difficult to judge: the wall of the crater visible in the distance is actually some 50 miles away from the rover.

On Aug. 12 NASA once again drew a bead on our closest planetary neighbor, as the Mars Reconnaissance Orbiter (MRO) lifted off from Cape Canaveral. The probe will reach Mars orbit in March 2006, take six months refining its flight pattern around Mars, then begin its mission, employing six scientific instruments to examine the Martian terrain in unprecedented detail. The MRO's most important goals: to learn more about the history and distribution of water on Mars and to evaluate landing sites for future robot explorers.

NASA—AP/WIDE WORLD

No Wonder

Aspirin and vitamin E are not quite the wonder drugs everyone hoped they would be, according to two July reports from the respected Women's Health Study. Regular use of each does not, for the most part, prevent cancer or heart disease in middle-aged women, although men 40 and older can take "baby aspirin" (81 mg) to help ward off heart attack.

Gimme Some Skin

One of the hottest shows touring U.S. museums in 2005 featured 25 human cadavers, flayed of their skin, all preserved using a special invisible polymer. "Body Worlds," which toured Los Angeles, Chicago and Philadelphia, places the see-through bodies in various poses—playing basketball, practicing yoga, riding a bicycle—to show in detail how the human organism works. Not everyone is thrilled with the exhibit, the brainchild of German anatomist Gunther von Hagens. When the show toured Europe before coming to the U.S., two British Parliament members condemned it as "unacceptable in a civilized society," and the Lutheran Church deemed it immoral. But record-breaking U.S. museum crowds seemed to enjoy the opportunity to view the innards of the human body as never seen before.

The Missing Link in Dinosaur Dining

On May 4 scientists unveiled a new fossil find that helps explain how dinosaurs made the transition from small, agile meat eaters to elephant-size vegetarians. The new star is *Falcarius utahensis,* a 125 million-year-old critter with 5-in. claws and spoon-shaped molars; adults were 12 ft. long and stood 3 ft. tall. *Falcarius* belongs to a group of dinosaurs known as therizinosaurs, which includes the feathered dinosaurs found in China in recent years. Paleontologists have now uncovered some 90% of its bones.

> **Warming will also cause reductions in mountain glaciers and advance the timing of the melt of mountain snow peaks in polar regions.**
>
> —**OMITTED SENTENCE,** *in a draft of a report on global warming, from a section crossed out by Philip Cooney, chief of staff for the White House Council on Environmental Quality. The onetime oil-industry lobbyist resigned and was hired by ExxonMobil*

Drawing Board

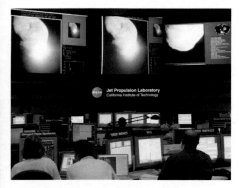

NASA's Smashing Success

Talk about fireworks: on July 4 the NASA spacecraft Deep Impact released an impactor probe that slammed into a comet, offering scientists a chance to study its makeup. Comets are believed to be among the oldest objects in the solar system.

Stem-Cell Breakthrough

On May 18, South Korean scientist Woo Suk Hwang announced that his team had created 11 human stem-cell lines perfectly matched to the DNA of 11 human patients. Scientists called it a giant leap toward creating custom stem-cell treatments for ailments ranging from Alzheimer's disease to severed spinal cords; opponents of cloning denounced the research.

The Fat Lady Sings for Atkins

How quickly we forget. In recent years millions of Americans embraced the Atkins diet, the nutrition plan cooked up by the late cardiologist Robert Atkins, which stresses a low-carb diet and casts bread and pasta as the enemies of slimness. But the fad seems to be over: on Aug. 1, Atkins Nutritionals, which makes more than 50 low-carb products and 200 nutritional supplements, announced that it was $300 million in debt and filed for bankruptcy.

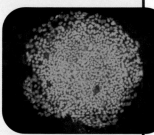

Uncle Sam Steps Up Efforts to Improve Nutrition

After four years of deliberation (and food-industry lobbying), the U.S. Department of Agriculture released its new nutrition recommendations in April. Out went the familiar black-and white pyramid encapsulating dietary guidelines; in came a rainbow-colored pyramid that sported a healthy-looking stick figure climbing a set of stairs, to stress the key role of exercise in maintaining overall good health.

The new food guidance system replaces the one-size-fits-all meal plan of the old pyramid with 12 different plans that promote an individualized approach to nutrition. The old plan, which measured food servings in inscrutable sizes, recommended the intake of large quantities of carbohydrates without drawing a distinction between nutritious whole grains and the highly refined carbohydrates that help us put on weight. The new plan stresses a diet rich in fruits, vegetables, whole grains and low-fat milk products. However, critics assailed it for not advising people to eat less, and for ignoring salt, saturated fat and cholesterol.

MyPyramid.gov
STEPS TO A HEALTHIER YOU

Arts

"KRUMP, CLOWN, BREAK IT ON DOWN!"
That's the refrain as krumping, the latest
face of hip-hop style, spreads like a
kinetic rainbow from the streets of South
Central Los Angeles to a neighborhood
near you. Break dancing on steroids,
krumping is frenetic, acrobatic and
mock-violent. That's Tommy the
Clown, a.k.a. Tommy Johnson, on the
right: a reformed drug dealer, the
Christian ex-con started the dance craze,
but he doesn't pretend he controls it;
there are now some 80 krump krewes in
L.A., which compete against one another
in dance-offs that Johnson hosts. Music-
video director David La Chapelle is
the scene's chronicler; his 2005
documentary *Rize* captures the
whump, thump and bump
of the best krumpers
in mind-boggling
full flight.

LAUREN GREENFIELD—VII

Paris Hilton

IS SHE THE LOVE CHILD OF A RED CARPET and a flashbulb, or did Paris Hilton spring full-blown from Andy Warhol's forehead? Either way, she is the pure creation of an age intoxicated with celebrity, famous for being famous, Zsa Zsa Gabor with a cell phone. Her art is her image; her talent is to pose and provoke, and she plays her role well. But the 24-year-old reality-TV star and heiress to the Hilton hotel fortune, who first came to wide attention as a dim figure in a sex tape circulated over the Internet, claims that change is coming to her glitzy, ritzy world.

Is Paris burning? Apparently so. The passionate party girl seems to own the phrase "That's hot." And early in 2005 she became engaged to the 27-year-old heir to a Greek shipping fortune who shares her first name, Paris Latsis.

Is Paris spurning? Yes, indeed. The fickle clothes-horse soon split up with Latsis, only to take up with the younger, wealthier heir to another Greek shipping fortune, 20-year-old Stavros Niarchos. But the young man apparently came to his senses after taking part in a party in a Las Vegas hotel that ended in a shambles. "I need time to reflect," he claimed he told Hilton as he broke off their relationship. "I should have been home today studying; instead, I am here paying $100,000 worth of bills." A commendable attitude, but as Vergil might have said: beware of Greeks baring rifts.

Is Paris yearning? Yes, indeed. She claims she's eager to shed her reputation as an heir-head and prove herself as an entrepreneur. Don't hold your breath. ∎

Mick Jagger

YOU SAY 60 IS THE NEW 40? DON'T TELL THIS gent: he seems to believe 62 is the new 22. Sir Mick—yes, he was knighted in 2003—led bandmates Keith Richards, 61, Charlie Watts, 64, and Ron Wood, 58, as the Rolling Stones launched their latest assault on the aging process and the wallets of elderly baby boomers everywhere. When they kicked off their 31st world tour and new album, both christened *A Bigger Bang*, at Boston's Fenway Park on Aug. 21, ticket prices ranged from $63 to $453. But no one seemed to be complaining: the new CD was hailed by a majority of critics as a strong return to form, and as for Jagger, no one has ever disputed that he is one of the greatest showmen of the age. His sheer vitality as he scampered across the giant three-story touring stage at Fenway left observers marveling. Nor has he lost his knack for sparking publicity from politics: the song *Sweet Neo Con* from the new album skewered George W. Bush's faith-based policies with the line: "You call yourself a Christian/ I think that you're a hypocrite."

What makes Mick tick? The kicks. He doesn't need the cash—according to *Billboard* magazine, the Stones have grossed more than $1.125 billion in ticket sales since 1989—but as Jagger explained long ago, he's addicted to the adrenaline rush he experiences in energizing a huge crowd. As he promised in mid-career, back in 1981: If you start him up, he'll never, never, never stop. ∎

Dave Chappelle

TALK ABOUT A RUNAWAY SUCCESS: IN MAY, ONLY WEEKS before the third season of his smash-hit comedy-sketch series *The Dave Chappelle Show* was due to premier on cable-TV channel Comedy Central, its eponymous star abruptly walked off the set and hopped a jet to South Africa. Left in his wake were his wife and two children; his agent; his publicist; and his writing partner, Neal Brennan—all of whom pleaded ignorance as to the comic's whereabouts—as well as the executives at Comedy Central, who had anted up millions to retain Chappelle's services after his first two seasons, outbidding NBC and FX.

Why all the fuss? Chappelle offers a fresh, satiric take on race, sex and pop culture that's often profane, sometimes profound, always provocative (especially on racial issues)—and very popular. The DVD of his Season One is the best-selling television-series DVD of all time. It should have been sweet vindication for Chappelle: after years of struggling, often in inferior vehicles, he had become the hottest, edgiest, most talked-about comic working today. Move over, Chris Rock!

Then again, that's quite a burden to carry: facing his third season, Chappelle must have felt like the Beatles at the height of their powers—how do you top *Sgt. Pepper*? When TIME's Christopher John Farley tracked the comic down in Durban (below), Chappelle told him, "I'm not crazy. I'm not smoking crack. I'm definitely stressed out." In a rambling interview, Chappelle blamed creative differences with Comedy Central execs for his shutdown but admitted that there was "a little psychological element to it." Brennan also expressed concern about his friend's mental health. The white-hot Chappelle, who soared to success by daring to take on some of the most hot-button issues in America's national psyche, may have flown too close to the flame—and the fame. ∎

Marin Alsop

Gender politics. When it comes to the arts, you'd think this touchy subject was ancient history—yet it lives on in the rarefied realm of classical music, where the Vienna Philharmonic was all-male until 1997, and only three of the top 75 U.S. orchestras had female conductors in 2005. So it was big news when the Baltimore Symphony named Marin Alsop, 48, as its new leader in July, and bigger news when word leaked out that the appointment had been strongly opposed by 90% of the symphony's musicians—or so claimed ensemble members on the search committee. After a painful deadlock, the orchestra members were rebuffed, and she was handed the baton. Later, Alsop addressed her new charges, asked for their support and offered to leave the room to let the musicians discuss their response among themselves. "I didn't even get back-

stage," the conductor told TIME. "They said, 'Come back!'"

Alsop has craved the baton since she first got the bug after seeing Leonard Bernstein conduct live when she was 9. In her 20s she worked as a freelance violinist in New York City; after hours, she would bribe her musician friends with pizza to let her lead them through Mozart symphonies. In 1984 she founded her own ensemble, the Concordia Orchestra, to ensure she would get regular conducting gigs. Eventually she got traction: she was named to lead the fledgling Colorado Symphony in Denver in 1993, then in 2002 became the first woman to head a major orchestra in Britain, as conductor of the Bournemouth Symphony. Despite her shaky start, don't look for her to conduct her restive troops with an iron hand. "This is the age of collaboration rather than autocracy," she says. ∎

OF PENGUINS AND LEMMINGS

While Hollywood's creative well runs dry, documentaries seize the energy in cinema

MARCH OF THE PENGUINS
Director Luc Jacquet's study of penguin peregrinations was plodding at times but captured Antarctica's eerie blue-and-white beauty

FOR HOLLYWOOD, 2005 WAS A SUMMER OF DISCONTENT. HOPES WERE HIGH that the Memorial Day weekend debut of *Revenge of the Sith*, the last installment in George Lucas' epic *Star Wars* series, would kick-start the year's busiest season at the nation's cineplexes. *Revenge* was indeed a hit, but as the weeks went by, one highly promoted extravaganza after another fell right off a cliff. By Labor Day, the results were in: attendance had dropped 11.5% from 2004, and ticket sales were down 9%. The bad news led to much pained analysis of what was ailing today's movies, and there was no lack of suspects. Many noted that Hollywood's target audience was—in TIME critic Richard Corliss's term—"dateless 14-year-old boys," leading to a glut of comic-book films such as *Fantastic Four* and *Batman Begins*. Others cited the endless cavalcade of remakes, as scriptwriters ransacked America's pop-culture attic and emerged with ho-hum updates of *Bewitched*, *The Dukes of Hazzard* and *The Longest Yard*. Or maybe it was the cell phones in theaters and all those prefeature commercials. By late August, the New York *Times* was quoting Hollywood execs as entertaining an even more daring conjecture: Could it be that too many movies … were just not good enough? Well, duh.

While Hollywood's offerings were marching, lemming-like, into oblivion, a very different trudge—that of the emperor penguins of Antarctica—turned out to be a surprise hit. The French documentary *March of the Penguins* enthralled audiences with its remarkable footage of the birds' arduous journey to ardor, shot under the most harrowing conditions. The film debuted at four U.S. theaters on June 24 and, like its subjects, just keep shuffling: by Labor Day, it had shown in 2,394 theaters and had become the No. 2 highest-earning documentary in history, behind Michael Moore's 2004 anti-Bush screed, *Fahrenheit 9/11*. Bulletin to Hollywood: if you put a fascinating film on the screen, people may actually pay to see it. ∎

CINDERELLA MAN Director Ron Howard's boxing film was cut to the pattern of 2003's hit *Seabiscuit*—nostalgia, feel-good vibes and big stars (Russell Crowe, left, and Renée Zellweger)—but it fell flat at the box office

REVENGE OF THE SITH The film, which traced the transformation of Anakin Skywalker (Hayden Christensen) into the evil Darth Vader, earned a strong $124 million in its first three days, but its glow didn't spread to other movies

HARRY POTTER AND *THE GOBLET OF FIRE* The fourth entry in the popular series was widely hailed as the best *Potter* film yet; after Hollywood's dismal summer, its success helped spark a livelier fall movie season

WE NIX SLICK FLIX, BUT HOT DOCS CLICK

While Hollywood's scripted sagas tanked at the box office, documentary films were offering precisely what the big special-effects extravaganzas lacked: subjects that were fresh, surprising, real and (gasp) entertaining. "We've kicked away the soapbox," *Murderball* co-director Dana Adam Shapiro told TIME. Call it docutainment. Among the year's best:

MAD HOT BALLROOM Marilyn Agrelo's fun, fresh look at New York City public school kids who take up ballroom dancing had audiences' toes tapping

ENRON: THE SMARTEST GUYS IN THE ROOM Alex Gibney's film skewered Kenneth Lay, Jeff Skilling, Andrew Fastow, above, and the other hustlers behind the crooked energy giant's Ponzi schemes

GRIZZLY MAN German master Werner Herzog used film shot by gonzo outdoorsman Timothy Treadwell, above, as the basis for this unnerving exploration of one couple's fatal obsession with killer bears

MURDERBALL Directors D.A. Shapiro and Henry Alex Rubin filmed the paraplegic athletes who compete in the Paralympics and emerged with an anti-*Rocky* just as tough as its featured players

GEORGE KRAYCHYK—UNIVERSAL

©LUCASFILM LTD. & TM

WARNER BROTHERS—ZUMA/CORBIS

FROM TOP: CLAUDIA RASCHKE-ROBINSON—PARAMOUNT CLASSICS; DAVID J. PHILLIP—AP/WIDE WORLD; TIMOTHY TREADWELL—LIONS GATE FILMS; THINKFILM

DANCING WITH THE STARS: John O'Hurley, a.k.a. J. Peterman from *Seinfeld*, proves that he is a man of élan; Evander Holyfeld's cha-cha was somewhat less exalted

DON'T TWIRL THAT DIAL

How to keep restless viewers glued in place? Network executives score with despairing housewives, hoofing has-beens and clueless castaways

UNREAL! IN 2004 FIVE OF THE TOP 10 NEW TV SHOWS were reality series, led by NBC's Trumpfest, *The Apprentice*. But in 2005 the tables were turned: the seven top new shows were all scripted. The big winner of the trend was ABC, which rebounded from years as the cellar dweller among the Big Three broadcast networks with two intelligent confections that combined hilariously far-fetched plot lines with enjoyable characters and crisp writing, *Desperate Housewives* and *Lost*.

Housewives, the most successful rookie show in years, served up a delicious blend of sex, scandal and soap-opera parody. It was certified as a national phenomenon when First Lady Laura Bush dubbed herself a "desperate housewife" in a humorous speech at an annual gathering of Wa-shington journalists. *Lost* was a riskier endeavor, a high-concept pairing of *Gilligan's Island* and *The X-Files*, but with writer-producer J.J. Abrams *(Alias)* in charge, the show proved a captivating mystery that made the most of its admittedly silly parts: monsters, polar bears (in the tropics), a mad Frenchwoman and a scary Canadian guy.

The year's final surprise was reserved for the summer season, when reality-TV reared its head (or feet) in another ABC hit, *Dancing with the Stars*, an unlikely mash-up of B-list celebrities (heavyweight Evander Holyfield, actress Rachel Hunter) and professional dancers. The show tapped into a surprising new appreciation of dance among Americans that was also reflected in the hit documentary film *Mad Hot Ballroom*. ∎

LOST The cast of castaways casts a longing glance at the horizon. Help was not on the way, but something even better—high ratings—did turn up

DESPERATE HOUSEWIVES Five veteran small-screen stars reigned over the mysterious, adulterous doings on Wisteria Lane: from left, Nicolette Sheridan, Felicity Huffman, Marcia Cross, Eva Longoria and Teri Hatcher

LEFT: MARIO PEREZ—ABC; TOP RIGHT: MOSHE BRAKHA—ABC

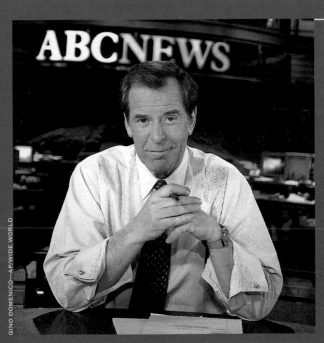

GINO DOMENICO—AP/WIDE WORLD

TOM BROKAW
NBC ANCHOR SINCE 1983
Brokaw retired late in 2004; alone among the Big Three TV evening-news anchors, he was able to enjoy a graceful farewell

PETER JENNINGS
ABC ANCHOR SINCE 1983
His death from lung cancer turned a spotlight on smoking, as the American Cancer Society and other agencies reported record numbers of new inquiries

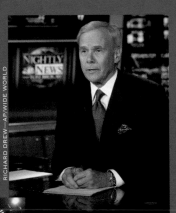

RICHARD DREW—AP/WIDE WORLD

HARAZ GHANBARI—AP/WIDE WORLD

DAN RATHER
CBS ANCHOR SINCE 1981
The Texan's farewell was clouded by the network's admission that the sources for an explosive 2004 *60 Minutes II* story on George W. Bush's National Guard service could not be verified

THAT'S THE WAY IT WAS

Tom Brokaw's departure from NBC late in 2004 ushered in a turnover at the anchor desks of four of the nation's most-watched news shows. Dan Rather retired from the CBS evening newscast in March; Ted Koppel plans to leave his post at ABC's late-night show, *Nightline,* in December 2005. Those departures were long planned, but on April 5, Peter Jennings, veteran anchor of ABC's evening newscast, announced on-air that he had lung cancer and would cut back his appearances; in fact, he never returned to the show and died on August 7 (see Milestones). The loss of the familiar faces had pundits wondering if the venerable news broadcasts could retain their audiences.

TED KOPPEL
ABC *NIGHTLINE*
ANCHOR SINCE 1980
Koppel never served as anchor of one of the major evening news broadcasts, but his long-running show was the only network news program ever to enjoy success in the late-night slot

BEBETO MATTHEWS—AP/WIDE WORLD

ON WINGS OF SONG

Classy star Kanye West provides the uplift as new hip-hop artists ascend to the heights (of the charts, anyway)

ANGELIC: West, often accused of being too much of a good guy for rap music, toyed with his image at the Grammy Awards ceremony

GRETCHEN WILSON Nashville's "Redneck Woman" kept her honky-tonk sound at the top of the charts with her fall CD *All Jacked Up*

BLACK EYED PEAS Dancefloor-friendly beats turned the mainstream hip-hop band's *Monkey Business* into a big hit, while singer-dancer Fergie's moves made them a sight to behold. From left, Taboo, Fergie, apl.de.ap, William

MAYBE IT WAS THE SUBJECT OF HIS INSTANT-CLASSIC single, *Jesus Walks*. Maybe it was the snazzy pair of angel's wings he wore at the Grammy Awards. Whatever the cause, when fans discuss Kanye West, one of pop music's biggest success stories of the past two years, the talk often sounds spiritual. "That record restored my faith in hip-hop," actor-singer Jamie Foxx said of West's monster 2004 album, *The College Dropout,* which went nearly triple platinum, topped all the major critics' polls, earned 10 Grammy nominations and made rap accessible to audiences that hadn't paid attention in years. In 2005 West did it again. His album *Late Registration* soared to the top of the charts on its release in late August, selling some 750,000 copies in its first week in the stores.

More *GQ* than gangsta, West is the unlikeliest of rap stars. As a producer, he had churned out hits for rap label Roc-A-Fella Records, but when he asked if he could rap on his own album, executives laughed: with his Gucci loafers, pink Polo shirts and college-professor parents, West was too soft, too bourgeois, too much a good guy to fit the image of the gangsta rapper. No problem: once West got the chance, he proved that audiences were ready for hip-hop music that dared to mix spirituality with skepticism and rap with gospel.

On *The College Dropout* West careered between Protestant hang-ups and urban gang-ups, revealing himself to be wise and stupid, arrogant and insecure, often in the same breath. On *Late Registration* he pushed further: one of the better-sounding rap records ever, it covers wide ground, from riffs on black college fraternities to West's newfound fame to racial oppression in Africa's diamond mines. And did we mention … you can dance to it? ∎

U2 Bono, the Edge & Co. were inducted into the Rock and Roll Hall of Fame, released a strong new album with a great single, *Vertigo,* and toured to adoring crowds

COLDPLAY Frontman Chris Martin, actress Gwyneth Paltrow's husband, led this four-man British unit to its biggest success yet with *X&Y*. The soaring riffs of the hit summer album were modeled on U2's stadium-sized anthems

David Hyde Pierce as a top-hatted Sir Robin, left, and Tim Curry as King Arthur, center, lead the cast of the Monty Python musical

THE INVALID REVIVES

A cavalcade of new plays and musicals brings a welcome pulse of fresh creative life to Broadway, the theater world's "fabulous invalid"

FOR MANY YEARS, BROADWAY SEEMED TO BE THE LAST colony of the British Empire, in thrall to the lavish productions of Andrew Lloyd Webber (and lest we forget, *The Phantom of the Opera* is still going strong after 17 years). Then it was the turn of the big musical-comedy revivals: *Chicago*, a semi-success in 1975, has been packing them in since a retooled version opened in 1996. In recent years, the focus has shifted to revivals of classic dramas featuring Hollywood stars *(see sidebar)*.

But here's the good news: this season's revivals were outshone by an unusually rich supply of new plays and musicals. The year's smash hit was *Spamalot*, Eric Idle's over-the-top update of the 1975 film classic *Monty Python and the Holy Grail*, which brought the zany British troupe's madness onstage intact, while adding some hilarious new numbers. *The 25th Annual Putnam County Spelling Bee* was a lighthearted hoot that proved (much like 2003's big hit *Avenue Q*) that audiences were ready for offbeat, low-budget productions. In more traditional terrain, *The Light in the Piazza*, with a book by Craig Lucas and music and lyrics by Adam Guettel, was widely called the best original American musical in years, and a late entry, *The Color Purple*, was hailed by many critics as lively and entertaining.

Happily, the trend included dramas, where strong new productions included John Patrick Shanley's probing *Doubt*; August Wilson's Tony-nominated *Gem of the Ocean* and Irish playwright Martin McDonagh's creepy meditation on storytelling and murder, *The Pillowman*. In short, the best sign that Broadway may be reviving is that it's no longer all about revivals. ∎

THE 25TH ANNUAL PUTNAM COUNTY SPELLING BEE The hilarious, low-budget send-up of six stellar spellers, by Rachel Sheinkin and William Finn, featured a witty book and lyrics rather than fancy sets

THE COLOR PURPLE TIME's critic loved this fast-paced musical version of Alice Walker's novel; the New York *Times* didn't. But, aided by a publicity boost from co-producer Oprah Winfrey, the show promises to be a hit

NEW YORK, NEW YORK, A HOLLYWOOD TOWN

One way to get bodies into the expensive seats on Broadway (and off-Broadway) is to put today's big stars in yesterday's war-horses. Three stand-out revivals are pictured below—and we didn't have room to show some of the other big-screen names who strutted and fretted on the New York stage in 2005, including Denzel Washington in *Julius Caesar*, Jessica Lange in *The Glass Menagerie*, Natasha Richardson and John C. Reilly in *A Streetcar Named Desire* and James Earl Jones in *On Golden Pond*.

GLENGARRY GLEN ROSS Alan Alda, center, led a fine cast that included Liev Schreiber, Tom Wopat and Gordon Clapp in David Mamet's 1984 portrayal of real estate hustlers, expletives not deleted

WHO'S AFRAID OF VIRGINIA WOOLF? Kathleen Turner and Bill Irwin won raves for their lacerating turns as Martha and George in Edward Albee's classic 1962 dissection of an academic marriage gone very sour

HURLYBURLY Bobby Cannavale, left, Ethan Hawke, right, Parker Posey and Wallace Shawn starred in a revival of David Rabe's pitiless investigation of ambitious sleazebags in decadent 1980s Hollywood

ArtsNotebook

STEPHANIE AND PETER BRANDT FOUNDATION, GREENWICH, CT.

❝ It's this reality. Like omigod, I have to tell the maid to buy diapers and get the pool boy to walk the dog? Can't I just make out with Kevin all the time? Being married sucks. **❞**

— **BRITNEY SPEARS,**
pop princess, complaining in Allure *magazine about playing stepmother to husband Kevin Federline's children*

Fresh Look at an Old/Young Master

As the 1980s took their turn on nostalgia's merry-go-round, a major retrospective of the colorful work of artist Jean-Michel Basquiat toured three U.S. cities. The show was a reminder that the Brooklyn-born Basquiat, whose mother was Puerto Rican and father Haitian, produced some irresistible work, as in *Boy and Dog in a Johnnypump*, 1982, above. Sadly, mediocrity and repetition dogged his last years, when his heroin addiction overcame his gifts and took his life. One sign his work is holding its value: an untitled work from 1982 sold in 2004 for $4.5 million.

JONAS EKSTRÖMER—AFP—GETTY IMAGES

Last Reel?

He's 87 now, but Ingmar Bergman, who devoted himself to directing plays in the early 1980s, returned to the screen with *Saraband,* a four-character chamber piece starring Bergman veteran Liv Ullmann. Said TIME critic Richard Corliss: "Sublime."

Watch Your Back, Eminem

The Beastie Boys proved long ago that rap music could be a gorgeous mosaic, and a new crop of unlikely rappers is taking hip-hop's concerns way beyond booty and bling. Native-American rapper Litefoot, left, deals his spiels in both Cherokee and English on his Reach the Rez tour. Hasidic hip-hopper Matisyahu, center, forswears rapping on the Sabbath, but his rabbinicalized reggae is surprisingly popular. Maxi Jazz, a.k.a. Maxwell Frazer, right, is a devout Nichiren Buddhist who leads the group named, of course, Faithless.

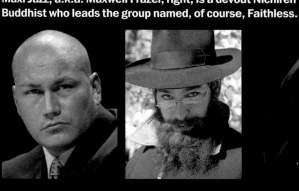

FROM LEFT: EVAN VUCCI—AP/WIDE WORLD; JIM COOPER—AP/WIDE WORLD; LAURENT GILLIERON—KEYSTONE—AP/WIDE WORLD

A Master of Droll, On a Roll

The actor who taught a generation how to rebel with a smirk has become a brilliant, understated master of pathos. Following up on his fine turns in *Rushmore* and *Lost in Translation,* in 2005 Bill Murray starred as the arrogant oceanographer in Wes Anderson's *The Life Aquatic with Steve Zissou* and as an aging ladies' man in Jim Jarmusch's *Broken Flowers.*

DAVID LEE—FOCUS FEATURES

Drawing Board

CONCERNED ELDERLY AGAINST DISMANTLING SOCIAL SECURITY

I WONDERED WHAT THE NEW ROLLING STONES TOUR WOULD BE CALLED ....

MIKE LUCKOVICH—JC

For Once, More Is More

Cincinnati, Ohio, 1963, above, is typical of the photographs of Lee Friedlander: it's crowded to the point of clutter, and it takes a while to realize it shows a bedroom suite in a store window, with the reflections of a lamppost and a church steeple over-whelmed by the commercial display. Friedlander, now 70, received a major retrospective (500-plus images) at the Museum of Modern Art in New York City; critics hailed his bustling frames as the work of a modern master of the American scene.

LEE FRIEDLANDER—COURTESY MOMA

Come Together

Who says you can't go home again? On July 2, a gaggle of pop musicians united—as they had at Live Aid in 1985—to rally against poverty in Africa. Once again it was Bob Geldof, now Sir Bob, who ran the Live 8 concert, which filled stages in 10 cities around the world. That's Sir Bob and Live Aid vet Sir Paul McCartney in the back. Mariah Carey, front left, was 15 years old in 1985.

LEFTERIS PITARAKIS—AP/WIDE WORLD

Cirque du Soleil's Latest Astonishment

NOTHING IS EARTHBOUND IN *Kà,* the new show from Cirque du Soleil, the Quebec City–based troupe, founded in 1984, that has crafted a highly popular new form of theatrical spectacle that's equal parts high-tech stagecraft and old-school circus acrobatics. *Kà* plays only in Las Vegas, in a theater specially built to suit the show, featuring side balconies from which the performers can fly over the crowd and two huge stages that materialize seemingly out of nowhere to lift, rotate, tilt and otherwise dazzle audiences. Some scenes occur in midair,

with the actors on wires or clinging to poles. As for the story of *Kà*—well, it involves good guys and bad guys, see, who do their best to chew the spectacular scenery before it chews them.

JOE CAVARETTA—AP/WIDE WORLD

Milestones

SWINGING INTO SLUMBER

For generations of Americans, the golf swing with which Johnny Carson ended his *Tonight Show* monologue was the most familiar of gestures, as smooth and easy-going as Carson himself; like a reverse alarm clock, the graceful move promised a restful sleep. The master conversationalist was a welcome presence in America's homes for three full decades. By the numbers, Carson was host of 4,531 shows, yakked with some 22,000 guests, weathered the competition of a slew of imitators, jump-started hundreds of careers, spent 35 years with Ed McMahon at his side, outlasted three wives and seemed to find happiness with a fourth. At right, he takes one final swing, on his farewell show in 1992.

JOSEPH DELVELLE—NBC—GLOBE PHOTOS

TOUCHED: Looking sheepish,
a rarity, Carson endures his fans'
acclaim on his final show

LEFT: DOUGLAS C. PIZAC—AP/WIDE WORLD; THIS PAGE, FROM LEFT: NBC—GLOBE PHOTOS; ALICE C. HALL—NBC—GLOBE PHOTOS; BETTMANN CORBIS; ALICE C. HALL—NBC—GLOBE PHOTOS

1925-2005

Johnny Carson

THERE WAS A WONDERFUL IRONY AT THE HEART OF Johnny Carson's career: the man most Americans felt they knew intimately was essentially unknowable in private life. Offstage, outside camera range, the great communicator and seminal talk-show host retreated into a shell. "He was great with 10 million people, lousy with 10," said his enduring sidekick, Ed McMahon.

Americans had a long time to get to know Carson: he presided over NBC's *The Tonight Show* for 30 years, a period that spanned the Cuban missile crisis and the fall of the Berlin Wall. A Nebraska native, he never lost the traits of the classic Midwesterner: he was boyish, low-key and down-to-earth, friendly yet reserved. Although he played host to the glitziest names in show biz, the glitter never seemed to rub off on him; he always remained the outsider, Our Man in Burbank, ever seeming thrilled that the big star of the moment had graced him with a visit—

BUDDIES: Carson and Ed McMahon first began working together in 1957

when, of course, the big star had likely moved mountains to secure a few precious moments on Carson's couch to plug her latest project.

Carson's mastery of both his medium and material seemed effortless; it

TRIBUTE: Carson's deadpan "Carnac the Magnificent" owed a debt to Jack Benny

wasn't. Illusion was his game: he took up magic as a boy, later saying it had been a way to combat his innate shyness. And "the Great Carsoni" became a fine magician, enthralling, among others, a young Dick Cavett, who would grow up to follow in Carson's footsteps. After serving a stint in the Navy in World War II, Carson earned a degree from the University of Nebraska; his thesis was titled, "How to Write Comedy Jokes." His idol was Jack Benny, and Carson was happy to acknowledge that he patterned his exquisite timing, mastery of the slow burn and ability to make fun of his own inferior material from Benny.

After a successful stint on an Omaha radio station, the 26-year-old Carson took his act to California in 1951, where he managed to garner a 15-minute live TV show in a terrible time slot: Sunday afternoon. But the show attracted the attention of Red Skelton, who hired Carson to write gags for his hit show and stand in as guest host on occasion. A failed quiz show followed; more damaging was the failure of his

1955 CBS talk-variety effort, *The Johnny Carson Show*, doomed by constant rejiggering and a still-tentative star.

To save his career, Carson left Hollywood and moved to New York City, where he finally found success in 1957 with the ABC quiz show *Who Do You Trust?* He also found McMahon—his enduring second banana, foil and one-man laugh track. Soon Carson was substituting for Jack Paar on *The Tonight Show;* this time around, his quick quips and easy command of the format made him the obvious choice to succeed the mercurial Paar.

Carson took over the show in 1962, and for three decades its basic format didn't change, although Carson succeeded in reducing its running time from 90 minutes to an hour, and in 1972 moved the show from New York City—an eternal butt of his gags—to California. The rituals were set in stone, offering what critic Kenneth Tynan called "the pleasure of the expected": there was Johnny's

ADIEU: A Bette Midler song brought Johnny to tears on his penultimate show

grand entrance, Ed's salaam of subservience, Paul Anka's blaring theme song, the monologue—often brilliant, often banal—and then the parade of skits, favorite characters and guests. Carson's show became a hothouse for gifted comedians: among those who first found fame on his stage are Bob Newhart, Woody Allen, Don Rickles, Rodney Dangerfield, Bill Cosby, George Carlin, Steve Martin, Roseanne Barr, Robin Williams, Jay Leno, David Letterman and Ellen DeGeneres.

Carson had his demons, but he beat a mid-career drinking problem. Thrice divorced, he turned his marital woes into joke fodder. He had three sons, one of whom, Richard, died in a 1991 car crash. His longtime smoking habit may have brought on the emphysema that killed him.

His timing sure to the end, Carson called it quits in 1992, and seemingly all America tuned in to watch his last shows. When he said his final farewell, he meant it: his last years were spent in the privacy he loved, enjoying his Malibu estate; his yacht, the *Serengeti;* and the company of his last wife, Alexis, 25 years younger. Old friends say he never stopped writing monologues on current events, ever the student of "how to write comedy jokes." ∎

RICHARD A. BLOOM—CORBIS

1925-2005

William Rehnquist

WHEN ASKED A CLASSIC QUESTION BY A PRIMARY school teacher in his native Wisconsin—what he would like to be when he grew up—young William Rehnquist answered, "I want to change the government." Although he followed a circuitous path (he had planned on becoming a college professor until an aptitude test indicated he would do well in law school), and although he endured years of solitary dissent on the U.S. Supreme Court (he was a strong conservative decades before the New Right appeared), Rehnquist achieved his goal.

During his 34 years on the court (the last 19 as Chief Justice), Rehnquist presided over a quiet revolution in which states' rights and police powers were steadily expanded, while the power of judges to interpret the Constitution expansively was significantly curtailed, as were some individual rights of U.S. citizens, such as the opportunity to appeal criminal convictions. In a poetic irony, the process Rehnquist set in motion, which was intended to scale back the Federal Government's power generally and judicial authority in particular, made the Supreme Court over which he presided vastly more powerful and important.

After serving in the Army Air Corps in World War II, Rehnquist studied law at Stanford University, working as a busboy in the school cafeteria to help pay his tuition. There he befriended and briefly dated a classmate and future Supreme Court colleague, Sandra Day O'Connor. After graduating first in his class (O'Connor was No. 3), he landed a coveted job as clerk to U.S. Supreme Court Justice Robert Jackson. In an early example of his staunch conservatism, the young lawyer tried without success to

him to the Supreme Court. In his early years, Rehnquist dissented from majority opinions so often (and so often alone) that his clerks jokingly gave him a Lone Ranger doll, which he happily displayed in his office. But as the nation drifted rightward in the years after Vietnam and Watergate, Rehnquist found himself less isolated. Following the election of Ronald Reagan, he sat squarely within the mainstream of public opinion, all without having budged an inch on the issues that mattered most to him.

When Chief Justice Warren Burger retired in 1986, Rehnquist was Reagan's natural choice as his successor. Along with the five other Justices appointed by Reagan and George H.W. Bush, Rehnquist was able to build a working majority that rewrote decades of liberal case law on subjects like the death penalty, affirmative action and lawsuits against government officials. In 1999 he presided over the U.S. Senate impeachment trial of President Bill Clinton, winning praise from both sides of the chamber for conducting the proceedings with strict impartiality. Little more than a year later, Rehnquist voted with the 5-to-4 majority in the divisive ruling that awarded the 2000 presidential election to George W. Bush.

Rehnquist lost battles as well. One of only two dissenters in *Roe v. Wade*, the 1973 decision that legalized abortion, he came within one vote of overturning that ruling in a 1992 case, *Planned Parenthood v. Casey*, but *Roe* remained on the books. In 1989, he found himself back in the minority in a decision that upheld the right of American citizens to burn their country's flag. Occasionally he surprised his conservative admirers. In 2000, he wrote for the majority in upholding the Warren Court's historic *Miranda* decision, which requires police to advise criminal suspects of their rights to an attorney and against self-incrimination. Through it all, his fellow Justices found unanimity on one point, commending the fairness and impartiality with which Rehnquist kept his divided court collegial.

In private, the Chief Justice was considerably more gregarious than his austere public persona suggested. He loved playing charades with his late wife Nan, three children and eight grandchildren; enjoyed singing old songs with friends; savored poker games with his fellow Justices and tennis games with his court clerks. A Gilbert and Sullivan fan, he also attended Handel's *Messiah* at holiday time for 50 consecutive years. He was a notorious gambling man, willing to place a bet on matters large and small, from the outcome of elections to how much snow would fall in the yard of the Supreme Court building.

Rehnquist was diagnosed with thyroid cancer in the fall of 2004; he hoped to remain on the bench through another annual term, or at least until the court's traditional opening date, the first Monday in October. But it was not to be. When he died in September, the man who had joined the court as its youngest judge had become its oldest member and one of the longest-serving Justices of all time. His longtime friend and colleague Justice O'Connor closed her eulogy with the words that the man she called "the Chief" had so often used to silence long-winded lawyers: "Counsel, the red light is on. Your time is up." ∎

persuade Jackson to vote against federal intervention to help integrate public schools in the landmark case *Brown v. Board of Education.* Rehnquist also lost his campaign to convince Jackson and the rest of the court that a rule automatically overturning criminal convictions based on coerced confessions should be abandoned. In a telling example of how Rehnquist waited for the country to come to him, as Chief Justice he wrote a majority opinion in 1991 ruling that coerced confessions were legitimate in cases where other evidence pointed to a defendant's guilt.

Yet this kind of vindication was long in coming. After his clerkship, Rehnquist settled in Phoenix, Ariz., where he became active in Republican politics; he returned to Washington to serve in Richard Nixon's Justice Department in 1969. Two years later, President Nixon nominated

1914-2005

General William Westmoreland

WILLIAM WESTMORELAND, THE GENERAL MOST CLOSELY identified with America's tragic misadventure in Vietnam, once lamented: "It was my fate to serve for over four years as senior American commander in the most unpopular war this country ever fought." If fate can make mistakes, it's hard not to imagine that Westmoreland didn't deserve his. Even as a youngster in South Carolina, "Westy" was so square of jaw and silver of hair, so soft-spoken and hard-willed, that friends called him "the inevitable general."

Westmoreland's distinguished combat record in World War II—he was decorated for heroism in North Africa and Sicily—sparked his meteoric rise. He was a colonel by 30 and the Army's youngest major general at age 42. By 1964, this confident, capable officer seemed the natural choice when President Lyndon Johnson sought a commander to do in Vietnam what Dwight Eisenhower and Douglas MacArthur had done in Europe and the Pacific a generation earlier: whip the enemy. But this was a different kind of war. Westmoreland's strategy of using massive numbers of U.S. troops to inflict unbearable losses on communist insurgents mattered little to an enemy that could replace soldiers faster than America's guns and bombs could kill them.

Through it all, Westmoreland's belief in eventual victory remained unshakable. He kept building up troop strength: there were 16,000 U.S. soldiers in Vietnam when he arrived in 1964; by 1967, there were more than half a million. But he also kept building up casualties, until Washington and the public no longer shared his confidence. After graphic TV coverage of the 1968 Tet Offensive made clear how far off victory remained in a war that Americans had been told for years would soon be won, Westmoreland was recalled to Washington and given a desk job. Four years later, after being passed over for promotion, he retired.

"As the soldier prays for peace, he must be prepared to cope with the hardships of war and to bear its scars," Westmoreland wrote in his autobiography. It was the tragedy of this man, who was born to lead, that the war he got wasn't the one he was prepared to cope with; it is the tragedy of all Americans that the hardships and scars of the most unpopular war this country ever fought still divide us. ∎

AP/WIDE WORLD

1938-2005

Peter Jennings

EXPLAINING THAT HE WAS TAKING A LEAVE OF ABSENCE TO combat lung cancer, ABC News anchor Peter Jennings told viewers in April, "I was weak," referring to the smoking habit he had kicked in the 1980s, then resumed briefly in the stressful days after Sept. 11, 2001. In truth, he was anything but. Jennings logged more than 60 hours on the air during the week of 9/11; he stayed on the air for 25 straight hours during ABC's coverage of the turn of the millennium. If Americans turned to Tom Brokaw for warm confidence or to Dan Rather for folksy feistiness, Jennings' audience tuned in for the news, delivered with authority. Viewers savored the strong jaw, soothing voice and impeccable wardrobe that inspired comparisons to James Bond, but Jennings didn't just play a journalist on TV; he was the real thing.

Born in Canada (he became an American citizen in 2003), Jennings had broadcasting hard-wired into his DNA. His father Charles was Canada's first national nightly news anchor, and Jennings was the host of a weekly radio program in Ottawa by the time he was 9 years old. Named ABC's evening news anchor at the tender age of 26, Jennings felt unprepared; he stepped down three years later and became ABC's chief foreign correspondent for the next 15 years. In the process, this man who had never finished high school transformed himself into an urbane expert on geopolitics. When he returned to lead ABC's nightly news show in 1983, Jennings offered a truly global report. A driven perfectionist, he found the strength to stop by his old newsroom a few weeks before he died in August. After a round of warm greetings, Jennings got out his pen and began editing the script for the evening's broadcast.

ANDREW KIST—REDUX

ENDURING: Miller in 1949; more than four decades later he said, "One of my joys in life is to see that what I've done has lasted"

AP/WIDE WORLD; INSET: W. EUGENE SMITH—TIME LIFE PICTURES

1915-2005

Arthur Miller

H IS PLAYS GAVE VOICE TO THE PLIGHT OF THE COMMON man, and Arthur Miller earned the right to pen them: he was born into a prosperous family in New York City, but when his father hit hard times during the Depression, his son's dreams of attending college gave way to a job in an auto-parts warehouse. Yet Miller persevered, and by the time he managed to graduate from the University of Michigan in 1938, he had already begun writing plays that dissected economics, the human heart and the ties that bind them. His first Broadway success, *All My Sons* (1947), portrayed a manufacturer of airplane parts who took his own life after his finagling led to the deaths of young airmen. Miller's art peaked early, with *Death of a Salesman* (1949), which he wrote in only six weeks. In the story of Willy Loman, the "low man" on capitalism's totem pole, Miller managed to create a classic tragedy for modern times; the play (right, with Lee J. Cobb as Willy) is likely to endure as long as live theater is performed.

Always a voice from the left, Miller refused to "name names" before the House Un-American Activities Committee in 1956; he had already exposed the folly of such witch hunts in *The Crucible* (1953). Later, after his unlikely marriage to sex goddess Marilyn Monroe ended in divorce, he mined the ruins for two plays and a screenplay. He kept writing into his 80s; his last plays did not succeed in America but were hailed by theater-savvy Britons. ∎

1915-2005
Saul Bellow

"I AM AN AMERICAN, CHICAGO BORN," DECLARES AUGIE MARCH, novelist Saul Bellow's alter ego, in the first line of the writer's breakthrough 1953 novel, *The Adventures of Augie March*. In fact, Bellow was neither American nor a Chicagoan: he was born Solomon Bellows in Lachine, a small town in Quebec, and he grew up poor in the slums of Montreal, the son of Russian Jewish immigrants. He was 9 years old when his parents moved to Chicago, which became his great tutor, great love and great subject. Bellow brought to serious American literature a fresh, hustling energy drawn from the streets, improbably but effectively yoked to a heady style; his novels are vigorous cocktails of call girls and the classics, Plato and payola. His masterworks, including *Augie March, Henderson the Rain King* (1959), *Herzog* (1964), *Mr. Sammler's Planet* (1969), *Humboldt's Gift* (1975), and *Ravelstein* (2000), trace the individual's quest for meaning in what he called the "nervous-making" 20th century. Along with Bernard Malamud and Philip Roth, Bellow put the lives of urban Jews squarely at the center of America's literary map, although he characteristically kvetched that he resented being linked with his two friends as "the Hart, Schaffner & Marx" of American letters.

Bellow was just as wised-up as his protagonists, a boulevardier in a Borsalino hat who was married five times. When he won the Nobel Prize for Literature, he declared, "The child in me is delighted; the adult is skeptical." The two adjectives are the ruling polarities of his work. ∎

HONORS: Bellows' "flashing irony, hilarious comedy and burning compassion" were cited when he was awarded the Nobel Prize in 1976

SALLY SOAMES—CAMERA PRESS—RETNA

ELEMENTS OF STYLE: "I hate to advocate weird chemicals, alcohol, violence or insanity to anyone," Thompson said, "but they've always worked for me"

1937-2005
Hunter S. Thompson

HE RAN WITH THE HELL'S ANGELS SO HE COULD WRITE about them—and ended up being badly stomped by them. He smoked too many cigarettes (and joints), drank too much, took way too many hallucinogens. He ran for sheriff of Aspen, Colo., under the Freak Power Party banner. He was portrayed onscreen by Bill Murray and Johnny Depp; he made the funny pages as Doonesbury's Duke. More important, Hunter Thompson was the creator of "gonzo journalism," his twisted take on the New Journalism of the 1960s. In Thompson's version—captured most notably in *Fear and Loathing in Las Vegas* (1972) and *Fear and Loathing: On the Campaign Trail '72* (1973)—the reporter not only participates in the events he covers but also gets seriously wasted while doing so, the better to cut through the fog of p.r. and pretense and touch a deeper, more insightful vein of truth. This was journalism as shamanism, and Thompson was its (very) high priest: at their best, his peerless rants open a window onto the dark side of the American Dream, his prose as careening and out-of-control as a teenager behind the wheel of a Thunderbird on a Saturday night with a six-pack riding shotgun.

Despite his outlaw persona, the Kentucky-born writer took his work seriously, keeping his archives and vast correspondence in careful order. A self-confessed gun nut, he took his own life with a pistol shot, emulating the suicide of a hard-living writing icon of an earlier era, Ernest Hemingway. But Thompson went Papa one better: he arranged to have his ashes shot out of a cannon after his death. ■

LOUIS PSIHOYOS—CORBIS

1925-2005
John De Lorean

HE WAS AN "ARROGANT EGOMANIAC," A VICTIM OF "THE deadliest sin ... pride." It's a harsh verdict, but that's the one John De Lorean passed upon himself after his freewheeling joyride as an automotive executive ended in a spectacular crash and he found religion. De Lorean's father, an immigrant, worked in a Michigan Ford foundry, and John grew up a gearhead, besotted with car culture. Hired as an engineer by Chrysler in 1948, he moved to General Motors in 1956; eight years later, as chief engineer at Pontiac, he crammed a huge engine into a small car he christened the GTO, creating the first "muscle car." He was head of Pontiac at 40, head of Chevrolet four years later.

De Lorean's lifestyle quickly became as supercharged as his cars; in staid Detroit, he drove a Maserati, grew his hair long, had cosmetic surgery, dated and married models and starlets. He left GM in 1972 to start up a new company; with backing from the British government, he began building his gull-winged De Lorean in Northern Ireland, but the futuristic, high-ticket car didn't catch on, and De Lorean was soon deep in debt. In 1982 he was arrested after being videotaped with a suitcase filled with cocaine, although he was found not guilty when his lawyer argued his client had been entrapped. Out of gas, De Lorean spent his last years exploring a new frontier: life in the slow lane. ∎

SPORTY: De Lorean and his namesake car, which was featured in the *Back to the Future* film series

ROGER RESSMEYER—CORBIS

CLARITY: Johnson said he would be remembered as the man who created the Glass House, below—and then, decades later, broke it, with his embrace of the frills of postmodernism

1906-2005

Philip Johnson

FORWARD-LOOKING ARCHITECT PHILIP JOHNSON WENT way beyond thinking outside the box; he brought the outdoors inside the box in the classic 1949 "Glass House" he built in Connecticut. Stripped-down yet elegant, the building owed a large debt to such pioneers of the modern style as Walter Gropius and Ludwig Mies van der Rohe. Johnson happily acknowledged his influences, and indeed his most lasting achievement may lie not in his own work but in his effective advocacy of the bracingly clean geometries of the founders of the Modernist movement.

In the 1930s the Harvard graduate used his pulpit as head of the Museum of Modern Art's architecture department to champion the new International Style, a term he coined. A master gadfly and promoter, Johnson was the Barnum of blueprints; he put architecture on America's cultural map, helped make Modernism the dominant style of the 20th century, then ushered in post-Modernism in the late '70s with his plans for the AT&T tower in Manhattan, capped with a Chippendale pediment. A favorite work was his Crystal Cathedral in California, whose airy glass walls evoked the edifice he said first made him fall in love with design: France's Chartres Cathedral. ∎

JESSE FROHMAN—CORBIS OUTLINE. INSET: EZRA STOLLER—ESTO

GREG WATERMANN—CORBIS OUTLINE

1931-2005

Anne Bancroft

SHE WAS ONE OF THE FINEST ACTORS of her generation, a leading lady of the Broadway stage whose superb performance as Annie Sullivan, Helen Keller's teacher in William Gibson's *The Miracle Worker,* was the stuff of legend. Yet in the topsy-turvy world of American pop culture, Anne Bancroft is best remembered for playing two supporting roles: as Mrs. Robinson, the aggressive older woman who seduces a young Dustin Hoffman in 1967's *The Graduate;* and, in real life, as the wife of funnyman Mel Brooks. Who said fame was fair?

Born Anna Maria Italiano in New York City, Bancroft claimed she scrawled "I want to be an actress" on a fence when she was 9. She learned her craft in the unforgiving crucible of 1950s live TV drama, then was discovered by Hollywood. After starlet roles in such B films as *Demetrius and the Gladiators,* she returned to New York City to star with Henry Fonda in *Two for the Seesaw* (1958), then triumphed in *The Miracle Worker,* repeating her stage role in the 1962 film. In her lengthy career, she played Brecht's Mother Courage, Golda Meir and Winston Churchill's mother, picking up five Oscar nominations and one golden statue, two Tonys, two Golden Globes and an Emmy along the way. So, here's to you … Anna Maria Italiano. ∎

CHARMER: "She was one of the most alive people I ever met," Dustin Hoffman told the Los Angeles *Times* after Bancroft's death. He was 30, she 35, when they starred in *The Graduate*

FRITZ GORO—TIME LIFE PICTURES

Jack Kilby
1923-2005

If you have ever used a computer, a cell phone, a microwave oven or an ATM, you have Jack Kilby to thank for it. None of these devices would be practical if not for the integrated circuit that Kilby invented in 1958. Within a few weeks of being hired by Texas Instruments, Kilby hatched the "Eureka!" notion of replacing bundles of expensive, erratic and slow transistors, resistors and capacitors by etching a single master circuit onto a chip of semiconducting material half the size of a paper clip. Always a prophet of the less-is-more approach, Kilby honed his induction speech into the Inventors' Hall of Fame to two essential words: "Thank you."

Shirley Chisholm
1924-2005

"My greatest political asset is my mouth," said Shirley Chisholm, the first black woman elected to Congress, "out of which comes all kinds of things one shouldn't always discuss for reasons of political expediency." After arriving in Washington in 1968, the Brooklyn community activist whose campaign slogan had been "Unbought and Unbossed" was assigned to the Agriculture Committee, which she interpreted as a deliberate slap to her urban constituents. "Apparently, all they know here in Washington about Brooklyn is that a tree grew there," she proclaimed. The House leadership eventually mollified her with a prized seat on the Education and Labor Committee. In 1972, Chisholm became both the first woman and the first African American to seek a major party's presidential nomination, losing the Democratic nod to George McGovern. "Someone had to do it first," she later reflected. After serving seven terms in the House, Chisholm retired in 1982, disillusioned that her party was "running for cover from the New Right." She emerged from retirement to serve as the U.S. ambassador to Jamaica during the first Clinton Administration.

CORBIS

Shelby Foote
1916-2005

In 1954 legendary Random House editor Bennett Cerf approached Shelby Foote, a novelist whose works were all but unknown outside his native South, to create a short history of the Civil War for that conflict's upcoming 100th anniversary. But like Topsy in *Uncle Tom's Cabin*, Foote's work "just grew." By 1974, when he wrote the last line with his vintage dipped-ink pen, the work encompassed three volumes, almost 3,000 pages and more than 1.5 million words. But Foote's labors remained largely unsung until 1990, when he starred as the narrator with the enthralling drawl for Ken Burns' PBS documentary series *The Civil War*. Asked to explain the storytelling spell he cast over tens of millions of viewers, Foote simply said, "I really did know what I was talking about."

PHILIP GOULD—CORBIS

George Mikan
1924-2005

Very few athletes have ever dominated a sport as George Mikan ruled the basketball court; indeed, he rewrote the game's rules. At 6 ft. 10 in. tall, he had almost no experience on the court when he tried out for the DePaul University team in 1942. After intensive training to build agility and coordination, he led the school to a 1945 NCAA championship, proving so invincible on defense that the NCAA wrote its goaltending rule to give opposing teams a fighting chance against him. When he signed up with the NBA Lakers, the pro league widened the "key" so that opposing shooters could get past Mikan and originated the 24-second shot rule because other teams would run out the clock rather than let him get his hands on the ball. In December 1949, when the Lakers played in New York City, the sign outside Madison Square Garden read simply, GEO. MIKAN VS. THE KNICKS.

Ossie Davis
1917-2005

Ossie Davis, who commanded a rich baritone, a piercing gaze and a quiet dignity, made both his life and his art a crusade for racial justice. Born in Georgia, Davis moved to Harlem to study acting and was drawn into the civil-rights ferment of the era. He and wife Ruby Dee (with whom he shared both a career and a 56-year marriage) served as M.C.s at Martin Luther King's 1963 March on Washington, and Davis delivered the unforgettable eulogy for his slain friend, Malcolm X, in 1965. He starred on Broadway (and wrote *Purlie Victorious*), on TV (*Roots: The Next Generation*) and in movies (seven Spike Lee films). "Any role you had was ... involved in the struggle for black identification," Davis reflected in 2004. "You couldn't escape it."

George F. Kennan
1904-2005

"The main element of any United States policy toward the Soviet Union," wrote an author identified only as "X" in the July 1947 issue of *Foreign Affairs*, "must be that of a long-term, patient but firm and vigilant containment." That last word came to define U.S. military and diplomatic strategy for decades after World War II. The man who coined the term, State Department official George Kennan, also foresaw the split between Soviet Russia and China, predicted the downfall of the Soviet Union 40 years in advance and advised U.S. policymakers that Vietnam was "a risky and profitless undertaking, apt to do more harm than good" years before others reached the same conclusion.

Frank Gorshin
1933-2005

Riddle us this: Who was widely regarded as one of the most gifted mimics of his generation but will most likely be best recalled for his campy romp as Batman's archnemesis on the 1960s TV hit? Great imposter Frank Gorshin found early fame imitating Kirk Douglas, James Cagney and the like, but his career peaked when he donned a question-mark-dappled green suit and emitted the squeaky, high-pitched giggle that became the Riddler's calling card. Gorshin returned to his roots in 2002, winning raves for impersonating George Burns in the one-man Broadway show, *Say Goodnight Gracie*.

Johnnie Cochran
1937-2005

He is best remembered for his "If it doesn't fit, you must acquit" doggerel in O.J. Simpson's 1995 murder trial, but attorney and civil-rights advocate Johnnie Cochran was prouder of the "No Js" he defended—people nobody cared about. His favorite case: helping set free Black Panther leader Elmer Pratt in 1997; Pratt had spent 27 years in prison for a murder he didn't commit.

Henry Grunwald
1922-2005

Grunwald loved two things: America (to which he and his family fled from Austria and the Nazis in 1938) and journalism. Named TIME's managing editor in 1968, he gave the magazine an overhaul in his 11 years at the helm, making it both more professional and less openly opinionated. In 1979 he began overseeing all Time Inc. publications—including FORTUNE, SPORTS ILLUSTRATED and PEOPLE—leaving in 1987 to become the U.S. ambassador to his native Austria.

Eddie Albert
1906-2005

On TV's *Green Acres* he played a city slicker who longed for the simple life, but in real life Eddie Albert was a complex man with a rich, varied biography: before World War II he was a spy for the U.S. military, then he became a war hero, awarded the Bronze Star for rescuing more than 140 trapped Marines during the battle of Tarawa. After finding stardom in movies and on TV, Albert worked for humanitarian and environmental causes; he was one of the first people to campaign against the use of the now banned pesticide, DDT.

Kenzo Tange
1913-2005

At the end of World War Two, the smoking ruins of Japan's cities were a tragic tabula rasa awaiting a design visionary bold enough to imagine his nation's rebirth. Architect Kenzo Tange was that man. His synthesis of traditional Japanese motifs with modern styles struck exactly the right balance for a country that needed to turn its back on the recent past but was unwilling to disavow its proud history. In the process, Tange created works of serene eloquence and beauty, as in his Museum of Asian Art in Nice, France, above. His Peace Memorial Park in Hiroshima is a haunting symbol of Japan's suffering and redemption, while his masterpieces—the twin, comma-shaped gymnasiums with innovative tensile roofs he designed for the 1964 Tokyo Olympics—are widely regarded as among the most beautiful structures of the 20th century.

Sandra Dee
1942-2005

When Stockard Channing's Rizzo sang "Look at me,/ I'm Sandra Dee,/ Lousy with virginity," in the 1978 film version of *Grease*, audiences got the joke, even though the real-life Sandra Dee hadn't starred in a movie for almost a decade. Like many of Hollywood's icons of youthful innocence, Dee's fame seemed a curse: the perky perfection of her teen-queen roles in the giddy *Gidget* and *Tammy* movies of the '50s and '60s concealed a tragic backstory. Dee would later claim to have been sexually abused by her stepfather from an early age, and she struggled with anorexia and substance abuse into adulthood. Her marriage at age 16 to singer Bobby Darin ended in a 1967 divorce, beginning a downward spiral in her personal life and career from which Dee never fully recovered.

Johnny Johnson
1924-2005

As immortalized in the song bandmate Chuck Berry wrote about him, *Johnny B. Goode*, pianist Johnny Johnson based his unique sense of rhythm on the trains that whooshed and clacked past his childhood home in West Virginia. A prodigy, he was playing the blues on local radio stations before he was 10. Johnson and Berry collaborated on hit songs that became primers for the new genre of rock 'n' roll: *Maybellene, Sweet Little Sixteen* and *Roll Over Beethoven*. They parted company as Berry's star rose and Johnson's drinking became a problem, but "Johnny B. Goode" savored some long-overdue recognition in 2001, when he finally was inducted into the Rock and Roll Hall of Fame.

Richard Pryor
1940-2005

He started out as a cute, rubber-necked stand-up comic in the mid-'60s, but Richard Pryor soon revolutionized the craft, talking about the things that mattered to him: sex, race (he defiantly used the taboo word nigger) and his own colorful, tumultuous life. And he dragged the culture along with him. He pioneered the feature-length comedy concert film and later starred in such mainstream Hollywood fare as *Lady Sings the Blues*, *Silver Streak* and *Stir Crazy*. His no-holds-barred comedy was fueled by a manic private life; his drug abuse climaxed in a 1980 freebasing incident when he set himself on fire. Multiple sclerosis silenced his later years.

Prince Rainier III
1931-2005

Europe's longest-serving monarch (56 years) ruled one of its smallest realms: Monaco consisted of some 400 acres when the Prince was crowned in 1949. Today it is some 20% bigger, thanks to land he helped reclaim from the sea. He married Hollywood star Grace Kelly in 1956, and together they transformed Monaco from a haven for shady customers into a thriving tourist haunt.

John Fowles
1926-2005

Influenced by Sartre and Camus, Fowles explored existential themes of obsession, uncertainty, chance and free will in such popular, critically acclaimed novels as *The Collector*, *The French Lieutenant's Woman* and *The Magus*. Artfully weaving his larger themes into his ingenious plots, Fowles stretched the limits of literary form; he was a master of the multiple ending. Never at ease with his commercial success, the writer lived largely as a recluse in Lyme Regis, England.

Simon Wiesenthal
1908-2005

An implacable, indefatigable agent of justice, Simon Wiesenthal was born in Polish Galicia, now a part of Ukraine; he survived incarceration in 12 different Nazi concentration camps during World War II. After the war, he provided information on war crimes for the Nuremberg trials, then founded the Jewish Historical Documentation Center, helping bring to justice hundreds of brutal wartime murderers. Sometimes controversial, he was accused of claiming others' victories in some cases, but his larger work earned the world's admiration.

August Wilson
1945-2005

Master playwright August Wilson had a feel for an electrifying ending. Wilson waited until after the May 2005 premiere of *Radio Golf*—the last installment in his epic 10-play Pittsburgh Cycle, a decade-by-decade chronicle of the African-American experience in the 20th century—to announce that he had inoperable liver cancer. The author of *Ma Rainey's Black Bottom, Fences* and *The Piano Lesson* was a high school dropout who educated himself in Pittsburgh's public libraries and worked as a porter, cook and dishwasher before turning to writing in 1965, in part because he had come upon a cheap typewriter. He went on to win two Pulitzer Prizes, a Tony Award and seven New York Drama Critics Circle Awards. His classic works will endure, and two weeks after his death, Broadway's Virginia Theater was renamed in his honor.

Eugene McCarthy
1916-2005

The Senator from Minnesota lost the election that made him famous, when he ran against President Lyndon Johnson in the 1968 New Hampshire Democratic primary. But by leading principled opposition to the Vietnam War, the former college professor persuaded Johnson to quit the race. McCarthy ran for the presidency four more times, to little note, but the sometime poet showed in 1968 that one courageous man could change history's course.

Frank Perdue
1920-2005

He was one of those unlikely masters of marketing who command our attention on the TV screen precisely because they seem to be untelegenic—and when it came to hawking chickens, it didn't hurt that Frank Perdue, with his beak of a nose, mournful gaze and bald head, looked as if he might have just emerged from an egg himself. Perdue took over the family business on Maryland's Eastern Shore in 1952 and slowly built it into a powerhouse, helping transform chicken farms from mom-and-pop outfits into gigantic agribusinesses. He galvanized his sales beginning in 1971, when he took on the pitch-man role for his broilers in a series of successful TV commercials.

Robert Moog
1934-2005

As a youngster, this son of an engineer and a piano teacher loved to tinker with the theremin, one of the first electronic musical instruments. By the time Moog was studying engineering and physics at Cornell University in the early 1960s, he had adapted the synthesizer—a bulky, expensive contraption that turned electric current into sound—into an affordable, portable, user-friendly instrument that allowed performers to mimic almost any sound in the world, and more than a few not of it. Soon music from Moog's synthesizer was turning up on Beatles albums, in Pepsi commercials and on the hit 1968 album *Switched-On Bach*. His contributions to modern music were recognized with a Grammy Award in 2002.

James Doohan

Shana Alexander, 79, witty, trailblazing journalist and author who gained fame by sparring with conservative James Kilpatrick on TV's *60 Minutes.*

John Bahcall, 70, avuncular astrophysicist and Hubble Space Telescope advocate whose pioneering work helped explain why the sun shines.

Lloyd Cutler, 87, consummate lawyer, mediator and Washington insider. A lifelong Democrat, the White House counsel to Presidents Jimmy Carter and Bill Clinton was widely admired by members of both parties.

Bob Denver, 70, perennially goofy sitcom star who found fame as beatnik Maynard G. Krebs on *The Many Loves of Dobie Gillis,* then went on to star as the lovable but inept first mate of the S.S. *Minnow* on *Gilligan's Island.*

James Doohan, 85, Canadian-born actor forever known (to his dismay) as chief engineer Scotty on TV's *Star Trek.*

Ibrahim Ferrer, 78, Cuban singer who found global fame late in life with the 1997 album *Buena Vista Social Club.*

John Garang, 60, Sudanese rebel leader turned Vice President and key negotiator of a fledgling peace agreement between the Islamist government and Christian rebels in the south. He died in a helicopter crash.

L. Patrick Gray, 88, onetime Nixon loyalist and acting director of the FBI during Watergate. He was forced to resign in 1973 after conceding he had destroyed papers belonging to Watergate operative E. Howard Hunt.

Edward Heath, 89, moderate leader of Britain's Conservative Party who, as Prime Minister from 1970 to 1974, brought Britain into Europe's Economic Community, today's E.U.

John Johnson, 87, rags-to-riches publishing entrepreneur who launched *Ebony* and *Jet* in the 1950s to inject positive images of African Americans into mass media—and succeeded.

Rosemary Kennedy, 86, oldest sister of President John F. Kennedy. Born mildly retarded, she was lobotomized at age 23; her plight inspired the Special Olympics, founded by her sister, Eunice Kennedy Shriver.

Virginia Mayo, 84, Hollywood blond of the 1940s and '50s who earned her greatest critical acclaim as Dana Andrews' cheating wife in the 1946 classic *The Best Years of Our Lives.*

Ismail Merchant, 68, producer half of the team that revitalized the literary, elaborately costumed period film. His life partner James Ivory was the director of their more than 40 screen collaborations, including *Howards End* and *The Remains of the Day.*

Rose Mary Woods

Peter Rodino, 95, unassuming Democratic Congressman who led the compelling House impeachment investigation of President Richard Nixon.

King Fahd bin Abdul Aziz al Saud, 84, monarch who kept Saudi Arabia stable during two decades of crises. He worked to open education to women and supported the 1991 Gulf War, even as he tolerated the terrorist-friendly brand of Islam known as Wahhabism. He had been largely incapacitated since a 1995 stroke.

Max Schmeling, 99, world-heavyweight boxing champion who became a reluctant symbol of Nazi might in the 1930s. In later life he befriended and lent monetary support to his great foe, American Joe Louis.

Jaime Cardinal Sin, 76, Roman Catholic Archbishop of Manila who used his moral authority to propel the "people power" revolts in the Philippines that brought down both the Marcos and Estrada presidencies.

Jimmy Smith, 76, organ virtuoso who pioneered a blend of jazz, R&B, bebop and gospel known as "soul jazz" and made the Hammond B-3 electric organ a respected jazz instrument.

James Stockdale, 81, candid and heroic Navy vice admiral who was a prisoner of war for seven years during the Vietnam War. He ran for Vice President on Ross Perot's ticket in 1992.

Luther Vandross, 54, smooth vocalist whose soulful ballads made him one of the most celebrated R&B crooners of his generation and won him eight Grammy Awards.

Rose Mary Woods, 87, doggedly loyal secretary to President Richard Nixon who took part of the blame for an 18-min. gap in a tape recording critical to the Watergate case that ended in Nixon's resignation.

Zhao Ziyang, 85, once the great hope of Chinese political reformers. He was purged from the party after he publicly sided with the 1989 Tiananmen Square protesters. ■